Bible Study Methods

Burton E. Brush

© Copyright 2023, 2019 by Reflections Publications
12001 Aragon Ave
St Louis MO 63138

ISBN # 978-0-9961441-1-7

First published in 1983 as a course for Pioneer Bible Institute.
Edited in 2023 and 2019 by Mildred Brush, Seth Folkers, Clayton Livengood, Elizabeth Spilger, Jonathan Spilger, and Kenneth Spilger

All Scripture quotations are taken from the King James Version of the Bible.

Printed in the Unites States of America

Dedication

Dedicated to **Burton E. Brush** who loved the study of God's Word so much and greatly yearned for others to share in this same love. He saw that many pastors and teachers of the Word needed the basics for *rightly dividing the Word of Truth* and proceeded to do something about it by creating this course on inductive study of the Bible. It is so basic that even the lay person and high school age students can use it.

Table of Contents

Purpose of this
Bible Study Methods Course

This Bible Study Methods Course was written for use in a class or study group but may be used for individual study. If you choose to do this study individually, please adapt the assignment instructions to your need. It would be wise to seek out a godly man (possibly your pastor) or woman who is a student of the Word of God to review your assignments with you after you have completed each of them.

We have also set up an email address for those doing individual study so that you may send assignments to a teacher of this study. The teacher can answer your questions, give help when needed, and guide you in your study. Our desire is that you succeed in this course so that your study of God's Word will be enhanced and you will be profited.

Email address: biblestudymethods1@gmail.com

Basic Materials Needed for this Course

If you do not have a computer, these resources are recommended for you to have in order to take this course (these would be good to have in your library with or without a computer):

1. **A Bible** — King James Version. This, and all other courses at the Pioneer Bible Institute use the King James Version for uniformity.

2. **A Strong's Concordance with the language dictionaries in the back.** This is now printed by various publishers. We recommended *The New Strong's Exhaustive Concordance of the Bible* published by Thomas Nelson Publishers.

3. *Expository Dictionary of New Testament Words,* by W. E. Vine is **recommended**, though not absolutely necessary. This is now also printed by various publishers.

4. *A Dictionary of English Words* — "Collegiate" dictionary or a copy of the "American Dictionary of the English Language"by Noah Webster (1828 Version).

All these are available electronically.

If you are using a computer, it is recommended that you have the above resources available to use and also some of the following:

Bible Software — there are many free Bible apps but we recommend one of the following: *e-Sword, Blue Letter Bible, Logos,* or *Online Bible.* These will make it easier to look up Strong's definitions. Most of these are simple to use.

"These hath God married and no man shall part;
dust on the Bible and drought in the heart."

— *Mile-Hi Evangelist*

Introduction of the Study

The Bible, as God's Word, is binding upon man and must be applied.

God gave us His Word so that we can know it to obey it.

But be ye doers of the word, and not hearers only, deceiving your own selves.

James 1:22

Bible study practices thorough observation.

Diligently study to know what God says.

Study to shew thyself approved unto God, a workman that needeth not to be ashamed, rightly dividing the word of truth.

2 Timothy 2:15

Chapter 1

Introduction of the Study

The Bible is God's very Word. It is an unique Book in every way. It is the only Book on earth which has God as its Author, and which is fully binding upon the souls, minds, and consciences of men. Since this book is God's Word, and since we are that part of His creation to whom this Book is written, it is essential that we be interested in understanding its contents.

In many places throughout the Scriptures we may find commands telling us to read those very Scriptures, that we study them, that we meditate upon them, that we apply them to our lives, and as well, that we proclaim them to the world. God has told us that it is His will for us to know His Word and that we know it well. No Christian is exempt from this heavenly requirement. Someday we shall all stand before Him and be judged according to this marvelous Book.

Beginning with our spiritual birth, we are told to desire the Bible: "*As newborn babes, desire the sincere milk of the Word, that ye may grow thereby*" (1 Peter 2:2). We can see from this passage that the Word of God provides us with the necessary spiritual food for our early spiritual growth. Then, as we grow, we will begin to "eat" the solid food: "b*ut strong meat belongeth to them that are of full age, even those who by reason of use have their senses exercised to discern both good and evil*" (Hebrews 5:14). Job said, "*I have esteemed the words of his mouth more than my necessary food*" (Job 23:12).

The Bible is a costly Book. Thousands of Christians have given their lives for the Bible in times past. We who believe the Bible today would likewise lay down our own lives for the same, should that be necessary.

The Biblical doctrine of inspiration is one of the great fundamentals of the faith. We insist that the *very words* of Scripture are inspired of God. This is a correct emphasis. If the *very words* are so important to us in the doctrinal sense, should these very same words not also be important to us in our study of God's Word and in our practice of that Word? Bible believers are definitely very conscientious and careful about the doctrine of inspiration.

God was not careless in delivering His Word into our hands. He carefully superintended the writing of the original manuscripts. He watched over these words down through the ages, when the vicious attacks of unbelief threatened to erase the Word of God from off the face of the earth.

Of course, we do not have the original manuscripts today. If they were now in existence, the *religious* world would have them enshrined somewhere, and people would fall down before those bits of stone, leather, or papyrus and worship them. As a consequence of that enshrinement and worship, mankind might have been denied the Scriptures for their God-ordained use in reading, and study, which results in obedience. God has preserved the Bible through persecution, fire, and flood. Do we dare be careless in our habits of reading and study as we labor to learn what God has to say to us through His Holy Bible? And, do we dare to interpret the sacred Scriptures in a flippant and reckless manner?

How may the preacher preach better sermons, the teacher teach better Bible lessons, and the Evangelist reach more lost souls? How can the Pastor build his people into fruitful Christians? This can be done only as each of these Christian workers gets to know God's Word *as* God has written it. They must know the *words* of Scripture, and they must know *all* of them. The preacher who knows his Bible well and who understands what it means will always have something to tell his audiences. He will be able to get "*honey*" from the "*Rock*" (see Psalm 81:16) to sweeten their souls. This is also true for the Bible teacher. The Bible is an inexhaustible Book, the absolute source of all truth, as well as being a very interesting and exciting book to read and study.

But is it sufficient to study the Bible only in order that we teach others? It must first be *applied* to the life of the proclaimer before that person is even eligible or prepared to proclaim that Word to others. The Bible is the only Book that is binding upon mankind, for it was inspired by the One True and Living God.

It would not do for us to neglect application in a study such as this. To do so would be to deny the very purpose of the Scriptures. It would be to see the Word of God only as a subject to be studied, to be analyzed in a mechanical and indifferent way. Since the Bible is not the same as other books, we must approach it in a manner befitting its uniqueness. Let us covenant with the Lord *right now* not only to learn *how* to study the Bible, but to begin a practice of studying it regularly. Let us also purpose to prayerfully apply each and every part of it to our lives. We must do all that we can to acquire much which will help us walk with the Lord in an ever new and vital way.

DIVISIONS OF BIBLE STUDY

A number of years ago, someone came up with a system of Bible Study which was built upon three questions:

1. What does it say?
2. What does it mean?
3. What does it mean to me – how can I apply it?

This has proved to be a very workable system for many Christians. It involves the three basic divisions of Biblical mastery:

1. **Observation**
2. **Interpretation**
3. **Application**

The courses offered in any Christian school to prepare people for serving the Lord fall into four basic categories. These are as follows:

1. **OBSERVATION** — What does it say?

   Bible Study Methods is the course which covers this area of knowledge at Pioneer Bible Institute.

2. **INTERPRETATION** — What does it mean?

   Biblical Hermeneutics and our course in Prophecy are courses which cover this area of learning. These are very important courses of study, for they analyze what the Bible says about *how* we must interpret it.

3. **APPLICATION** — What does it mean to me – how can I apply it?

   This is a matter of life and living for Christ, along with our service for Him. Personal devotional times, preaching services, practical Christian work, teaching opportunities all contribute to the application of God's Word to the life of the Bible student. While no single course is directed toward the application of God's Word to the life, *all* of the courses make a contribution to this in some way, whether directly or indirectly. Every believer must be very careful to apply the Word of God to his or her life personally FIRST, before making application to others.

4. **PROPAGATION** — How can I tell it to others?

> Teaching methods, Homiletics, Personal Evangelism teach how to proclaim the Word of God. The essential task of the Christian is to tell. We have *all* been commanded to be witnesses. We not only learn how to propagate in the classroom, but must practice this learning by doing it on a regular basis.

Each book of the Bible should be approached in a different way. It is also wise to approach the same book of the Bible in different ways. The Analysis courses of Pioneer each approach the Bible in different ways, using a Study Guide system. Bible Study Methods is a necessary prerequisite for most of these courses.

~~~

GUIDELINES FOR UNDERSTANDING THE SCRIPTURES

The Bible is a supernatural Book. It cannot be understood by the natural human mind (1 Corinthians 2:14). God must illumine the sacred page for us. 1 John 2:27 tells us of the Anointing of the Holy Spirit, Who is our Teacher. Whether we read and study alone in the privacy of our trysting place, in our living room, in our office, or if we "sit at the feet" of some Bible teacher or preacher, it is still this same Holy Spirit Who teaches us. We must recognize Him, and we must depend upon Him.

Later we shall see that we also must study the Bible in much the same manner as we would study any book. But let us now see some suggestions for a *spiritual* approach to God's Holy Word.

As we turn to the Bible, we:

(1) **BEGIN WITH PRAYER** — When the Apostle Paul was praying for the Ephesian believers, he did not pray for their health or their wealth. He prayed that they might understand spiritual things (Ephesians 1:16–19). Spiritual knowledge comes through the Scriptures as they are taught by the Holy Spirit.

The publishers of nearly all of the more recent versions are almost blasphemous when they claim that their particular version will enable one to understand God's Truth. The illumination of God's Truth is a work of the Holy Spirit alone. No man dare lay claim to it.

God is our Teacher — 1 Corinthians 2:12–14

We can ask God's help — Read John 16:12–15 and 14:26. Our prayer should be, "*Open thou mine eyes that I may behold wondrous things out of thy Law*" (Psalm 119:18).

(2) **READ THE BIBLE ITSELF** — Someone asked a great Shakespearean scholar years ago, "How do you study Shakespeare?" His answer was clear, "Read Shakespeare."

G. Campbell Morgan wrote some wonderful books on the Bible. It is said of him that he would not put pen to paper to begin writing until he had read a particular book of the Bible through 50 times. If we are to get the facts of the Word of God, we must keep on reading it (Deuteronomy 17:19; Revelation 1:3). How easy it is to turn first to the commentaries, or to devotional books, before looking at the Scriptures themselves. How much we miss by doing this! God wants to speak to us directly from His blessed Book.

(3) STUDY THE BIBLE — Although we **must** read, reading alone is insufficient -we must study (2 Timothy 2:15). "Inspiration is 95% perspiration," said G. Campbell Morgan. We cannot learn mathematics through a "devotional reading" of the mathematics book! Many people substitute devotional reading of the Bible for STUDY. This will not work.

There are three wonderful facts which justify that we study the Bible thoroughly and seriously:

-1. God gave the Bible.

-2. The Bible waits to be studied diligently.

-3. God gives us that which is necessary for a study of the Bible. Thus, the most simple of us can understand God's Word if we study it.

John Wesley was said to have been a man of one Book. He arose from his bed at four and five o'clock in the morning every morning to read his Bible. He read it in five different languages. You had better believe that this is one very effective method of studying the Word of God! But suppose you can read the Bible in but one language. Why not give yourself to a mastery of the Book in that language?

(4) MEDITATE ON THE BIBLE — As it was profitable for Israel to meditate on the Law of God (Deuteronomy 6:6–9; Psalm 1:1–2; Joshua 1:8), it would also be exceedingly profitable for us to ruminate the Word constantly. In order to do this, we must either practice memorization or constant, repetitive study. Or better yet, both study *and* memorize.

(5) MEMORIZE THE BIBLE — See Psalm 119:11. This is a very important way of getting the Word of God into our hearts and minds so it may have an influence upon our lives. Memorization takes much time and effort. However, anyone can do it. We knew a man in his late 70's who was memorizing in Revelation chapter 19. He had memorized all of the New Testament up to that point, and was determined to complete it all before the Lord took him home. In a memory contest in our Church in Nebraska, the first prize was won by a dear lady who was nearly 80 years of age.

(6) APPLY THE BIBLE — Obey it! If we do not obey the clear commands of God, the Bible will become a closed Book to our understanding. The Bible is meant to be obeyed, and we are meant to obey it (James 1:22). There is but one Biblical way of showing our love to the Father and to the Son. This is by obedience (see John 14:21).

"I am now reading the Bible and behaving it," said the Chinese student. There are two aspects to obedient Bible study:

-1. The assimilation of Scriptural Truth makes Bible study worthwhile. Not only does the Bible reveal life, but it shows us how to live.

-2. The appropriation of Scriptural Truth leads to increasing light. Failure to appropriate (obey, live) leads to spiritual blindness and atrophy (read Mark 4:23–25).

(7) BE REVERENT TOWARD THE BIBLE — The Bible student must never allow himself or herself to become too "familiar" with the Word of God. That is, we must never be *casual* about this blessed Book. We must reverence it. We must "take off our shoes" (spiritually) every time we study it (Exodus 3:5). It speaks to us of a Holy God, and it demands holy lives of us.

-1. Reverence makes reception possible. Mark 4:1–20 teaches us this fact.

-2. Reverence involves a prayerful dependence upon the Holy Spirit to teach us and to illumine the Truths He wants us to know.

-3. Reverence involves coming to a holy God as an undeserving sinner because of God's mercy and grace.

～～

THE BIBLE IS PRACTICAL

Profit — 2 Timothy 3:16–17 speaks to us of the Word of God being profitable (useful, beneficial) that the "*man of God may be perfect, throughly furnished unto all good works.*" We must study for benefit, for our own profit in a practical sense. We are often all taken up by the "iotas," while the boundless dimensions of great Scripture Truth are ignored. Problems do exist in the Scriptures, and they must be solved, but it is not the parts of the Bible we do not understand which should take up most of our time. We must major on the parts that we do understand. These demand our obedience. Bible study must be profitable, not merely theoretical and theological.

Experience — The Bible is a Book of human experiences as well as one of doctrinal Truth. It is not only a record of the spiritual experiences of others who lived long ago, but it shows us experiences which can and must be our very own. Not only that, but much of the Bible can only be understood by us as we *experience* God's Truth. God teaches at times through suffering, through joy, through His comfort. We can best understand God's faithfulness when we have personally experienced it. Our Bible is no abstract text on a theoretical religion, this Book is a living Record of dynamic experience. It is *real* and it is *practical!*

Study Questions

1. Which version of the Scriptures do we use in this course?

2. What do we say the Bible doctrine of inspiration includes?

3. By what supernatural means do we understand the Scriptures?

4. What are the four divisions of Bible study?

5. Explain each of these four divisions.

6. List the 7 guidelines for understanding the Scriptures.

7. Since the Bible is practical, what must we be careful to do as we study?

8. Since it is a book of human experiences, what should that mean to us in a practical sense?

Men's books with heaps of chaff are stored,
God's Book doth golden grains afford;
Then leave the chaff, and spend thy pains
In gathering up the golden grains.
                                        —*Anonymous*

Overview of the Study

Observation practices Inductive Bible Study.

God gave us His Word so that He could change our life to fit it, not change it to fit our life.

Ye shall not add unto the word which I command you, neither shall ye diminish ought from it, that ye may keep the commandments of the LORD your God which I command you.

Deuteronomy 4:2

Chapter 2

Overview of the Study

The purpose of this study is to teach inductive Bible study and to give practice in it. Various approaches and methods will be presented. Every attempt will also be made to direct the student toward a genuine reverence for the Word of God, while that student is learning how to study. The importance of care and accuracy in your study will be emphasized.

The words of the Scriptures are important to the Bible student. We must consider both *each* word and *all* the words.

> *"Every word of God is pure: He is a shield unto them that put their trust in Him. Add thou not unto His words, lest He reprove thee, and thou be found a liar."*
>
> — *Proverbs 30:5–6*

> *"Ye shall not add unto the word which I command you, neither shall ye diminish ought from it, that ye may keep the commandments of the LORD your God which I command you."*
>
> — *Deuteronomy 4:2*

Does it make any difference whether we add or subtract the words of the Bible by tearing out pages, denying the Truths of the Bible, or by carelessness in our reading, study, or interpretation? It makes no difference at all! Regardless of how we do the adding or subtracting, the message is changed, and the meaning is not as God intended it to be. God's words are precious. The blood of tens-of-thousands of martyrs has been shed for the defense of the Bible. Let us be exceedingly careful with this blessed Book!

Methods can too often become ends in themselves rather than being the means to a greater end. We must be watchful about this. The method is of no value unless it produces the fruit of the knowledge of the Word of God. This knowledge must then in turn produce the fruit of righteousness. There are many involved and complicated methods of Bible study. One such method which we have seen could easily lead one to produce a notebook full of almost useless charts and analytical diagrams without necessarily giving the student a better grasp of God's Truth.

The end result of all Bible study should be, "*That I may know Him*," Jesus! And to know Him is to love Him. To love Him is to obey Him and to serve Him.

This Course of Study Will Involve

Basic structure:

(1)   Words (or terms)
(2)   Sentences
(3)   Paragraphs

The instruction presented in this course of study covers the basics to all methods of Bible study. We must know the meanings of the words of the Bible. We must know how to understand the statement of a passage — what it actually says. We must also be able to determine the central theme of a paragraph, a chapter, and a book of the Bible.

Which brings us back to our beginning question: "What does it say?" We must determine the statement of a passage of Scripture if we are to understand the Bible. Our use of the basic principles taught here will lead us to a knowledge of the Word of God. The Word of God will in turn transform the life of every Bible student "*by the renewing of* (the) *mind*" (Romans 12:2).

Other methods of Bible study will be built upon the basic principles that we will be studying. Then, as the years pass, and as the experiences of life multiply, the student will find that one or more of the many methods of Bible study are best suited to his or her particular temperament. Also, the methods and approaches used will vary from time to time, in accordance with the needs or area of interest at any given time.

Inductive Bible Study

What is *inductive* Bible study?

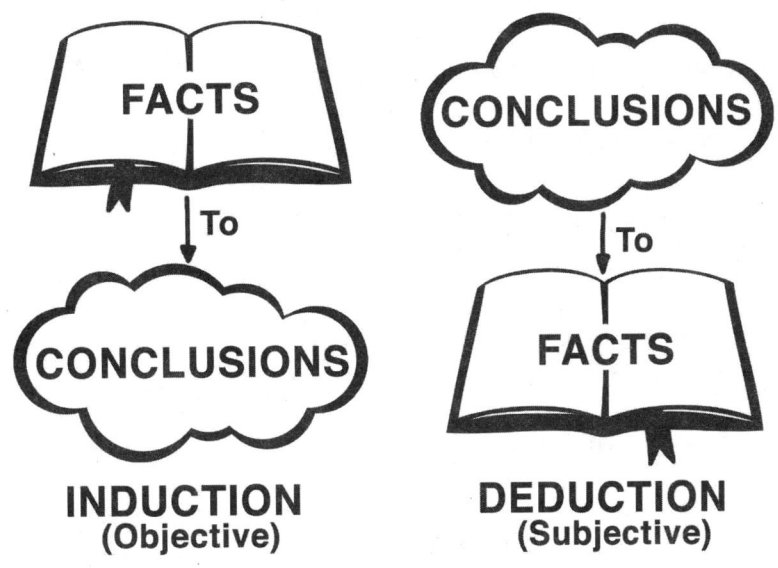

The Deductive Method (You speak to the Bible to support your beliefs.)

The deductive method is one of the most commonly used. It is legitimate for the Christian to use, but its use must be limited to certain kinds of studies.

In deductive study the student assumes a conclusion for which he or she then finds proof texts from the Bible. Another way of stating it is, you go to the Bible to prove your beliefs. The student begins with generalizations and moves for their support to the particulars (or proofs). By its nature, deduction tends to be subjective and prejudicial. It can produce those who dictate to the Scriptures rather than allowing the Scriptures to dictate to them.

At times, doctrinal studies or topical studies will utilize the deductive method, though induction is the safest route. Too many people assume a belief and then try to reinforce that belief by searching for supporting passages of Scripture. The cults use this method. By taking a disconnected part of a passage, or by twisting a word or two, they believe that they lend truth to their falsehoods. Bible believers must never practice this method in this way.

As human beings we enter this world with no knowledge of anything. Everything we know must be learned. We can only learn about God from the Bible. That will involve inductive study.

The Inductive Method (The Bible speaks to you to establish your beliefs.)

Inductive study is firsthand study. It starts with the facts from the text and draws a conclusion. In its purest sense, it assumes no knowledge or prejudice to begin with, but it carefully studies the Scriptures expecting God to speak and show them the Truth. Some of the more prominent characteristics of inductive study are seen as follows:

(1) It lets the Bible text or passage speak for itself.

(2) It observes first, then it interprets and applies.

(3) It analyzes what the Bible says (content), and how it says it (form or structure).

(4) It is aware of explicit and implied Truths.

(5) In it, original, firsthand study holds a prominent place.

You need to learn these five characteristics.

Again, let us contrast induction and deduction: "Induction is the logic of discovery, while deduction is the logic of proof."[1] In practice, however, the two methods are mutually dependent. A Christian does not usually begin a study of the Bible in an entire vacuum. There will be at least a few basic assumptions. This is to be understood. For efficient, honest study, then, deduction should only *supplement* induction at every point. We must always be conscious of the fact that it is not our privilege to "pour the Word of God into a mold of our own making," but rather it is our responsibility to allow the Word of God to mold our thinking into God's pattern.

If the Truths of the Bible already resided in man, there would be no need for a Bible. There would be no need for Bible study. However, God has given us this blessed Body of Truth simply because mankind has a need for it. This Truth, we repeat, is not in man. It comes from an external source — God. Man, left to himself, goes astray from God and righteousness. Man is a source of error and confusion, not of Truth. Only the Bible, God's Word, can bring Truth and order into the world of mankind.

Three Facts about the Inductive Method

It Is Scientific in Approach

The truly scientific approach is to see things *as they really are*. Induction observes first, then it concludes, rather than seeking support for its prejudiced conclusions.

Much of the so-called science of our day consists of coming to anything with a deep prejudice, e.g., evolution or uniformitarianism in science. All real evidence and facts are made to fit into those preconceptions. This has also become true in the discussion about Greek texts. The more influential institutions have rejected the *Textus Receptus* offhand. The time for discussion is past as far as they are concerned. All dissenters are branded "extremists" of some sort.

Its Process Consists of Analysis

The common tendency is to *first* gather all of the aids possible to be used in helping us to do our seeing and thinking. This is a flight from the Bible into the works of men. Its result is a secondhand knowledge which is dead in the pulpit or the classroom. It does little for the life of the student.

In inductive study, the student analyzes the minute parts of the Scripture, while at the same time looking at its larger parts. It analyzes the words, the construction of sentences and paragraphs, it looks at the context and even at the punctuation. It consists of an analysis of the Bible itself. The result of this is excitement, vigor, and fruitfulness. The Word itself has power (Heb. 4:12). An excellent approach in preaching or teaching is given in Nehemiah 8:8, where they read the Word distinctly, they gave the sense of the passage read (explanation), and they caused the people to understand the Word of God.

Its Purpose is to Discover

What do we discover?

> (1) What did the original authors (God and man) intend to say for their time as well as for our day?

> (2) What did these authors (God and man) mean?

> (3) Am I willing to subject my body, soul, and spirit to that Message? This means submission and obedience.

Discovery of any kind is exciting, whether it is the discovery of a new land, of a precious mineral deposit, of a significant ancient document, or of a wonderful spiritual Truth in the Bible. The excitement is very real to the discoverer. Of course the excitement of spiritual discovery far exceeds that of all other discoveries, for the spiritual finds have real value in the life which now is and the life which is to come.

Conclusion

Direct, independent Bible study is a *must*. We need the fruits of our own study and discovery more than the gleanings of another in their commentaries, helps, messages, etc. We need to know *for ourselves*. We must have direct, *firsthand* contact with the Scriptures. We need *personal* discovery.

Of course, commentaries are valuable, but they must be kept in their place. They must not be used before our direct study. The Word of God is the only Book which we may read without questioning what it says. All of the writings, messages and comments of men must be studied with a measure of skepticism. We must always place a question mark above the writings and sayings of even the most dependable of men, for we know that all of mankind is fallible and subject to error. We ought not to merely reject the conclusions of men offhand, but we must subject them to a comparison with the Word of God. God's Word alone is the measure by which all Truth is determined.

I was privileged to have heard the preaching of Dr. Harry Ironside on a few most memorable occasions. He was a wonderful Bible scholar and preacher. The great Moody Memorial Church in Chicago used to fill to its capacity each time he preached there, and I would do my very best to be among that great number. I have a number of his books in my library, and hope to someday have them all.

However, just because I respected Dr. Ironside and his preaching does not mean that I regard him as having been infallible in all that he spoke or wrote. We may not accept his words as being without probable error. He too was human, and we must even read with care whatever that great man wrote. Ironside was undoubtedly right in the great majority of what he said and wrote. However, we do not mean to say that we must have a suspicious skepticism toward all men. We simply emphasize the fact that we must regard *only* the inspired Word as being our infallible guide. How thankful I am that I had this fact emphasized to me early in my Christian life, for it has kept me from following some men into error. We must learn to practice suspended (deferred) judgment and weigh all teaching against the Bible itself.

You must study to be changed. You must purpose to obey even before you embark upon any study of God's Word. Do not simply study in order to satisfy your curiosity. The Bible is not like a museum through which we may pass as tourists looking curiously at the exhibits. The Bible is binding upon the souls and lives of men and women. It is God's message addressed to us!

[1]*The Bible in the Making of Ministers*, Charles Eberhardt, Association Press, New York, page 130.

Study Questions

1. Why must we be sure to read the Bible carefully and accurately?

2. What is the aim of following any method in our study of the Scriptures?

3. What must we avoid in the use of any method?

4. What does this study involve? (Three items.)

5. Explain induction.

6. What are the five points given under induction?

7. What three facts do we present about the inductive method.

8. Explain deduction.

9. In what cases is each method (deduction and induction) used?

10. Why must we emphasize what the Bible says over what men say about it?

(About the Bible)

This Holy Book I'd rather own
Than all the golden gems
That e'er in monarch's coffers shone,
Than all their diadems!

Nay, were the sea one chrysolite,
The earth a golden ball,
And diamonds all the stars of night,
This Book were worth them all.

For here a blessed balm appears,
To heal the deepest woe;
And he that seeks this Book in tears,
His tears shall cease to flow.

—Selected

[This poem appeared in the publication of the Gospel Mission of South America
— May - June, 1974.]

God's Unchanging Word

For feelings come and feelings go,
  And feelings are deceiving;
My warrant is the Word of God,
  Naught else is worth believing.

Though all my heart should feel condemned
  For want of some sweet token,
There is One greater than my heart
  Whose Word cannot be broken.

I'll trust in God's unchanging Word
  Till soul and body sever:
For, though all things shall pass away,
  His Word shall stand forever.
                              —*Martin Luther*

Methodical Bible Study

Observation begins with terms.

**Study to know each term as it is used in context of the literary form
and atmosphere of the passage.**

*But he answered and said, It is written, Man shall not live by bread alone, but by every
word that proceedeth out of the mouth of God.*

Matthew 4:4

Chapter 3

〜

Methodical Bible Study

I n order to study the Bible productively, one must use method. Involved in methodical, inductive Bible study is a system (or systems) of approach, of development, and of drawing conclusions. While the details of actual procedure may vary from day to day, as well as from passage to passage, the *basic* forms and approaches are much the same. Let's consider some thoughts about method in Bible study.

1. **Definition of Method:**

   "Method denotes orderly, logical, and effective arrangement of one's ideas for an exposition or an argument, or of the steps to be followed in teaching, *in investigation* … or in any kind or piece of work."[1]

   "Methodical Bible study, then, is concerned with the proper *path* to be taken in order to arrive at Scriptural truth. More specifically, it involves the discovery of those steps necessary for achieving its goal and their arrangement in a logical and effective manner."[2]

2. **The Nature of the Inductive Method:**

   The inductive method is direct and independent in nature.

   (1) Direct — Our methods must turn to the Bible as the basic Textbook, and not to books *about* the Bible. Such methods place primacy upon firsthand observations. This has been covered.

   (2) Independent — Spurgeon mentioned that "two opposite errors beset the student of the Scriptures: the tendency to take everything second hand from others, and the refusal to take anything from others." By independent we mean free from the use of commentaries. Commentaries (the works of others) are important, but they must be used only in *their* proper place– that is, *after* we have done our very best to make a thorough study of the Scripture passage for ourselves.

3. **Requisites in the Use of the Inductive Method:**

(1) **Thoroughness** — In thoroughness, we determine all of the facts. Although no one method may be thorough in itself, the use of method or system will generally produce thoroughness in time. Lack of any method can never be thorough.

-1. We must use every helpful **means** at our disposal to determine the facts of Scripture.

-2. As to the **scope** of our study, there must be a lifetime goal of complete mastery of the Scriptures, although it is not truly possible for one to completely master the Bible in one lifetime, or in many lifetimes. However years of patience and persistence will pay off. Remember, this goal should not be just for the "professional" Christian workers. It is for every Christian.

Halfway measures are no good. While some may settle for a superficial glance, those who would be faithful with God's Word, and who would walk with Him, will examine it carefully. God has in mind the very best for us. He desires that we dig it out carefully. We should have a healthy fear of not being careful enough in our Bible examination. We need never be afraid that a passage will ruin some idea of our own.

Every Christian must realize the Bible's inexhaustible supply of Truth and blessing. It may be likened to a cool, refreshing artesian well. No matter how much we drink out of that well, there is always more. We may return again and again to the same passage and still find more and greater truths and blessings. Familiarity does not breed contempt when it is a reverent familiarity with the Word of God. Familiarity brings blessings multiplied.

(2) **Consistency** — This means that the same or similar methods are used each time we turn to the Bible. Conclusions are thus based upon more nearly equivalent considerations and processes. Of course, different sections of the Bible are approached in a different manner. However, there must be the same thoroughness as we study every part.

The Bible student must be patient and persistent. They must never give up! Every Christian must develop habits of *regular* Bible study, and they must be consistent about these habits. We should make it a rule to not speak about a passage unless we have taken the time to study and understand that passage well.

We once had an adult Sunday School teacher who would not study his lesson. "I'm not much for studying," he said. He would let each person read and comment on a verse, followed by a discussion. He never drew any conclusions, and one opinion was considered to be as good as another. I called this "the sharing of ignorance."

(3) **Mental Discipline** — People are not naturally adept at reasoning. This is especially true in our day. We must work hard to develop a logical turn of mind. The use of consistent method is one of the very best ways of doing this.

We must learn to think. The end of this study is not simply to learn methods. It is to have our minds trained to think. Thinking is not easy, and it does not come naturally to most of us. Methods are a means of developing that necessary ability to think systematically and thoroughly.

-1. We must not be afraid to ask questions of the Word of God, but we must be careful to allow the Word of God itself to answer those questions. We need to look at it hard, and allow it to ruminate in our minds.

-2. We need to think with variety. It is not the aim of this study to provide a precise and rigid formula for Bible Study. Each person differs from all others, in background, in education, and in personality. Each part and passage of the Bible is different and unique in itself. We must learn to use system utilizing organized variety.

(4) **Honest Sincerity** — We can have no pretensions as we study the Bible independently and openly. We must come with the honest purpose of wanting the Bible to speak to us, and we must be willing to conform to its commands and challenges. God opens His Book only to the sincere and willing mind and heart.

The Bible is no "mystical" book in which we find some magical words and phrases which carry hidden suggestions of meaning. The Bible is written in standard grammatical and literary patterns (i.e., the sentence, the paragraph, etc.). The laws which govern the study of all other writings in the English language also govern our study of the English Bible. Words and their meanings, grammatical constructions, context, etc. must play an important part in our study of the Bible.

The Language of Our Study:

We study in our own familiar language best of all. Since we think most clearly and ably in our mother tongue, it is best suited to our study. Yet, we must realize that the Bible was first written in Hebrew, Aramaic, and Koiné Greek. What we have is an excellent translation, but it is a translation nonetheless. Something is always lost in translating from one language to another. For example, the English word "of" has 11 definitions in our copy of Webster's unabridged dictionary. "For" has 27 definitions in the same dictionary. In Ephesians 4:12 the word "for" appears 3 times translated from two different Greek words — the first one being *pros,* and the next two being *eis.* It stands to reason that the Greek word translated "for" in each case would aid us in understanding which of the 27 English definitions is meant.

The fact that something is lost in translation is a result of the judgment of the confusing of tongues recorded in Genesis chapter 11. Yet, without doubt, God has intervened in the translation of the Bible which we use in this study. He has remarkably aided the translators. It is amazing to see and contemplate the accuracy of the King James Version of the Bible.

This writer also reads somewhat stumblingly in the ancient Spanish version of the Bible. Such a reading may call our attention to a certain word or phrase, but the most profitable study is in my King James Version.

We now come to **OBSERVATION**.

Observation

As mentioned earlier, the four divisions of Bible Study are:

> (1) Observation
>
> (2) Interpretation
>
> (3) Application
>
> (4) Propagation

This course of study has to do with OBSERVATION. The aim of methodical Bible study is to *observe carefully.* Observation is a process of search and discovery, of analysis and conclusion, of study and development.

1. Definition and Purpose of Observation:

Observation is "the act or faculty of … taking notice; the act or result of considering or marking attentively."[3]

Observation is seeing things as they *really* are, not as we think them to be. It involves our seeing with an unbiased eye; impartially, openly, intelligently. This lays the foundation for accurate interpretation.

Observation of the Scriptures goes further. It has to do with the *spiritual* "eyes" ("*the eyes of your understanding*" Eph. 1:18). It transcends purely physical sight involving merely *sensory perception.* It does, however, require that we use our physical eyes to see, the mind to reason, and the hands to write down our observations. It is a human act, but it must be divinely motivated, directed, and illumined. This incorporates the physical and the spiritual. It has to do with *spiritual comprehension* and *obedient response.*

2. **Requisites of Observation:**

(1) We must have the *will* to know God's Word. It demands a strong desire. When men and women really *want* to know God's Word badly enough, they will apply themselves earnestly.

We sincerely believe that God gives a hunger to know His Word. That hunger is often seen in new converts. We are also commanded to desire the Word of God (I Pet. 2:2-3). We cannot please Him without faith (Heb. 11:6). Faith is believing God, and God speaks to us through His Word. "So then faith cometh by hearing, and hearing by the Word of God" (Rom. 10:17). For that reason also we must be careful that we study God's Word carefully.

(2) We must be *prayerful* in our observation. Psalm 119:18, "*Open Thou mine eyes, that I may behold wondrous things out of Thy Law."*

(3) We must be *careful* and *exact* in our observation. Carelessness is a serious error. Many false teachings have come from carelessness in the study of the Bible.

*An example of this was seen by a friend in Chattanooga. A Pastor, chiding the teachers in his Christian school, read Proverbs 18:9 as follows, "He also that is slothful in his work is a **bother** ...." He stopped short, and proceeded to berate those teachers for their supposed slothfulness. Even the small school children detected his carelessness. What a sloppy example. No wonder his teachers all quit that year.*

(4) We must be *persistent* in observation. This has been mentioned before. Giving up on a problem passage early will never bring us to a satisfactory knowledge of the Scriptures.

3. Analysis of Observation:

The four main components of any Biblical passage are:

(1) Terms — This covers words and their meanings.

(2) Structure — This includes sentences, paragraphs, segments, and books. This consists of the relations and interrelations between terms, or more specifically, the grammatical construction of the text.

(3) Literary form — That would be prose, poetry, allegory, etc.

(4) Atmosphere — This means the underlying tone, mood, or spirit of a passage. This requires that we become familiar with various kinds of background information. Examples: *Paul wrote Philippians and other of his Epistles from prison. Jeremiah prophesied to a rebellious Judah and suffered much persecution.*

4. Observation of Terms:

(1) Definition of a *Term* —

"A term is a given word as it is used in a given context." A term, therefore, has but *one* meaning, whereas the same word may have several meanings as seen in a dictionary apart from a context.

Example: *"Trunk" could mean part of a tree, an elephant's proboscis, a box, or a chest. "Spring" could be the season of year, to leap, a spring of water, etc.*

Let us be sure, then, to determine the correct meaning of each *term* in each passage that we study. Each *term* has but one meaning. This is determined by definition, context, atmosphere, etc.

Take note: *You can save a lot of precious time in doing word studies if you determine the context first and then follow the definition which fits.*

(2) Kinds of Terms —

−1. *Routine* and *Non-routine* Terms

- ***Routine:* These are terms whose meaning is at once obvious.** There is no need to do a word study. The meaning is clear.

- *Non-routine:* **These are terms which should be especially noted and researched.** It is well to record these (make a list) as you read or study and look them up in one of the helps. This will be covered in detail later.

There are three classes of *non-routine* terms:

1) Terms which we do not understand, or which are difficult to understand.

2) Terms which are crucial to a correct understanding of the passage. Also, this includes those terms which, though not crucial, are nevertheless significant for understanding the clear statement of the passage.

3) Those terms which otherwise express profound concepts. The curiosity of the student must ever be active.

Note: The distinction between routine *and* non-routine *terms is intended to help the student develop discretion. Each student may occasionally differ with other students as to what he or she would consider to be a routine or a non-routine term, depending upon need, education, understanding, etc.*

Students will frequently follow "rabbit trails" out into the woods and lose sight of the main path *of the study. The most common "rabbit trail" is doing too many word studies. Some have looked up almost every word in the passage. On the other hand, others will simply look up enough words to fulfill the assignment and overlook the most crucial terms which would aid them in understanding the passage.*

–2. *Literal* and *Figurative* Terms

- *Literal:* These are terms which should be interpreted according to the letter, and which are meant to convey their primary or usual meaning. Most terms which are in the Bible should be taken in their literal sense. The Bible is not an allegory, and it is not to be taken allegorically.

- *Figurative:* These are terms which are symbolic, and which express a secondary idea distinct from their original meaning. This does not mean that the student is free to spiritualize and allegorize any and all passages, but that some terms and connected passages are intended to be symbolic by the Divine Author of the Scriptures. Every one of these will be very evident to the student of the Bible.

It is very important to be aware of this distinction if a valid interpretation of Scripture is to be made.

Reading along one day, I came across the following statement: "Genesis 1:20—Salient: it gives the date of the First Advent in regards to eternal life as a 'gift' after the resurrection. The word 'life' occurs AFTER four thousand years (four days: see Genesis 1:19). Verse 16, by the way, gives you the date of the birth of Christ and the Second Advent of Christ. It will be between September 20th and 23rd." Now, that is allegorizing at its worst. And this was by a man who advertises himself as a Fundamentalist. Many people follow this man.

   –3. The *Identity* and *Inflection* of Terms —

    1) *Identity:* Terms may be identified by use of the following grammatical categories: nouns, pronouns, verbs, adjectives, adverbs, prepositions, conjunctions, interjections, and articles. It is important that we be able to identify each of these.

    2) *Inflections:* An inflection is a change of form in the terms to indicate case, gender, number, tense, person, mood, voice, etc. This would include the conjugation of verbs, the declension of nouns, pronouns, and adjectives. It is important that we have the ability to note the inflections of terms.

    Note: *Someone once suggested that it is dangerous to make word studies in the original languages without considering the inflections. We maintain that it is not dangerous, because we already have our English Bible.*

    Most students who have a basic knowledge of the English language should have no trouble with the inflections of the English words in our Bible. However, a knowledge of the languages of the Bible would be necessary for the student if he or she is to consider the inflections of the words looked up in the course of making a word study. We accept the inflections in our English Bible. Let it be sufficient for us to limit our study to only the word meanings and draw the inflections from the King James Version.

  (3) Tools for Identifying Bible Terms —

We must work to develop our English vocabulary. The King James Version has many words which are not used commonly today. These have been labeled *archaic* words. *Archaic* means "belonging to an earlier period; ancient." These words have ceased to be used in conversing or writing by society in general. *Archaic* does not mean obsolete. We do not discard the great classics of literature just because there are a few *archaic* words in them. We learn what those words mean, so we can understand what the writers of that literature were saying. The King James Version was translated in 1611, though there have been two or three minor revisions — mostly in spelling. Many of the words have changed their meanings in recent years, and some words have been dropped from the common vocabulary of our day. With the poor quality of education being given today, the English language is changing and deteriorating more rapidly, probably, than at any other time in history.

–1. *The English Dictionary:* Many *archaic* terms may be identified by simply using a reliable Collegiate English Dictionary or, if possible, get a copy of the "*American Dictionary of the English Language*" by Noah Webster (1828 version). The dictionaries included in most computers and phones won't have the needed volume to be helpful in many of these studies. It would be wise to get one of the recommended dictionaries either as a hard copy or as an app for your computer. Some Bible software includes the 1828 dictionary.

   Example: *"Meet" – "[Now Rare] suitable; proper; fit." Our office dictionary (unabridged) gives five definitions for the word "meet." The Bible meaning is covered in the first of these. It is an adjective. See Genesis 2:18, 20.*

–2. *The Exhaustive Concordance of the Bible,* by James Strong, S.T.D., LL.D, originally published by Abingdon. *The New Strong's Exhaustive Concordance of the Bible* published by Thomas Nelson Publishers is an excellent edition.

   This is the most important one volume for any Bible student apart from the Bible itself. You can look up passages in the Bible and many other necessary things if you have an exhaustive concordance.

   Strong's is based upon the *Textus Receptus* and the *King James Version.*

   • Work in this study is based upon *Strong's Concordance.* The step by step use of this reference book in doing studies of words is described as follows (*not on a computer*):

   Suppose you want to look up "*conversation*" found in 1 Peter 1:15.

   1) Begin in the main concordance. Notice how the pages are designed. Look

under "conversation." You will note, "*so be ye holy in all manner of c…*," and to the right of that is the number *"391."*

2) You now turn to the back of *Strong's Concordance,* to the "GREEK DICTIONARY OF THE NEW TESTAMENT," and find number *391.*

3) You will see that there is the word in Greek letters, then it is spelled out in English letters in such a way that we can pronounce it. Following that is the definition, *"behavior:—*conversation."

4) Take careful note of the ":—" symbol in every definition. The words following the ":—" symbol are not the definition, but the *usage* in the King James Version. The King James translates the Greek *anastrophe* as "conversation." That is simply it.

- The student should become familiar with the abbreviations, symbols, and signs which Strong has employed in his two dictionaries. These are given at the beginning of each dictionary in the back of the book.

–3. Next in line for the student is *Vine's Expository Dictionary of New Testament Words,* by W. E. Vine. This is a tool which every serious Bible student should have. First, you must have a *Strong's Concordance,* for it is difficult to use *Vine's* without it.

It is necessary to use *Vine's* in connection with a *Strong's Concordance,* unless you are familiar with the Greek language and have a Greek New Testament. However, even then, it is wise to check with a *Strong's Concordance* to find which Greek word is used for example with the word "HONEST, HONESTLY, HONESTY." There are 2 adjectives, KALOS and SEMNOS. There are 2 for adverbs, KALOS and EUSCHEMONOS. And there is one noun, SEMNOTES. How would you know which Greek word is translated "honest" in I Peter 2:12 if you could not consult your *Strong's Concordance?* The number is *2570* and is KALOS. You can see it as an adjective in *Vine's.*

It is unfortunate that Mr. Vine, a Britisher, generally follows the critical Greek texts whenever differences in the texts occur. He also tends to place too much credence in the RV (English *Revised Version,* long ago discredited), but we merely ignore his references to it. After all, we are seeking definitions. This is another reason why it is vital that you use your *Strong's Concordance* which is based upon the King James and the *Textus Receptus* (received text or traditional text) of the Greek New Testament which is superior to the critical texts, such as Nestlé's, the Westcott and Hort text, and others.

–4. Helps by other writers — there are a number of these helps which are available; some are quite helpful, others are less so. Among these are the following:

1) *Theological Dictionary of the New Testament,* by Geoffrey W. Bromiley, Kittel and Friedrich, editors — This is the abridged, one-volume edition published by the William B. Eerdman's Publishing Company. Again, you must use the *Strong's Concordance* to find the Greek word used, but the words are very easy to find, and the definitions are clear.

2) *The Interlinear Greek-English New Testament,* by George Ricker Berry. This is the *Textus Receptus* Greek New Testament. It will help us to know the changes made by Hort and others. The English translation is written above the Greek text, with the King James translation appearing in columns alongside. To use this effectively requires that the student learn the Greek alphabet and its English letter equivalents. **Note**: This particular book is hard to find.

Interlinear is also published as "The Interlinear Literal Translation of the Greek New Testament" by Thomas Newberry. This is the same interlinear information, but lacks George Ricker Berry's lexicon and notes.

3) *Word Pictures in the New Testament,* by A. T. Robertson. It is in 6 volumes. He was an avid follower of the critical texts. However, I have found a little help from time to time in these books.

4) *Word Studies in the New Testament* by Marvin Richardson Vincent. This is a New Testament study help. This resource is especially good for how concise it is in its definitions and comments.

5) There are many helps that can be found on the web or can be downloaded to your computer. Among them are: *e-Sword, Blue Letter Bible, Logos,* and others. These will include many tools to help in your study.

(4) Determining Meanings —

The meanings of terms may be determined by the following steps:

−1. Find the meaning of the word in the original language (Hebrew, Chaldee, or Greek) using the helps mentioned above.

−2. Study the immediate context in which the word is found in the passage under consideration.

−3. Study the usage of the word in the book which you are studying, in all of the writings of that human author, and in the Bible as a whole.

−4. Look at all the occurrences of the Hebrew or Greek word in the Bible. How was it used in the context of those occurrences?

Note: The meaning of the word is not necessarily the meaning of the *term*. Some words have various meanings, as may be readily seen in a Hebrew or Greek dictionary. As was mentioned earlier, a *term* has but *one* meaning. We may determine that meaning by using the three steps shown above.

(5) When using the computer tools —

The meanings of terms may be determined by the following steps although the software apps may vary:

−1. Look up the verse using the format within that app that has the Strong's numbers attached to each word.

−2. Click on the Strong's number attached to that word to find the definition in Strong's. If there is a resource to find the usage of the word, go to that as well so you will have the correct form and word definition. We are looking for accuracy not just a definition.

−3. Often within the apps there will a source that will give all the occurrences of that word found in the Bible.

Note: See Appendix 2 for a guide to preparing a deeper word study with the intention of preaching and teaching.

[1] *Methodical Bible Study*, by Dr. Robert A. Traina, Asbury Theological Seminary.

[2] Traina, op. cit.

[3] *Webster's Collegiate Dictionary*, Fifth Edition.

Assignment

Find the meaning of each term:

1. Look up the words indicated below in *Strong's Concordance*.

2. You may do your work on this sheet or on a separate sheet of paper or notebook.

3. Always write the number of the word first, and write the Greek word in English letters.

4. Once you are finished looking these word up in your *Strong's Concordance*, look these words up in your *Vine's Expository Dictionary* (see page 45).

Strong's Concordance

From the book of Philemon —

1. (v. 1)   fellowlabourer

2. (v. 6)   communication

3. (v. 6)   effectual

4. (v. 7)   bowels

5. (v. 8)   enjoin

6. (v. 8)   convenient

7. (v. 10) begotten

8. (v. 11) unprofitable

9. (v. 10) Look up "Onesimus"

From the book of Romans —

10. (1:1)   called

11. (12:1) Beseech

12. (12:2) transformed

Vine's Expository Dictionary

From the book of Philemon —

1. (v. 1)   fellowlabourer

2. (v. 6)   communication

3. (v. 6)   effectual

4. (v. 7)   bowels

5. (v. 8)   enjoin

6. (v. 8)   convenient

7. (v. 10) begotten

8. (v. 11) unprofitable

9. (v. 10) Look up "Onesimus"

From the book of Romans —

10. (1:1) called

11. (12:1) Beseech

12. (12:2) transformed

Study Questions

1. What is meant by method?

2. What is the nature of the inductive method? (Two things.)

3. What are the four requisites in the use of the inductive method?

4. Why is mental discipline important for the Bible student?

5. Though we study in the King James Version, why is it important that we know the Hebrew, Aramaic, or Greek word from which the English word was translated?

6. What are the four divisions of Bible study?

7. Define observation and give its purpose.

8. What are the four main components of observation?

9. What is a "term"?

10. What is a routine term? What is a non-routine term? Why do we distinguish them in this way?

11. Why must most parts of the Bible be taken literally?

12. List the tools for identifying Bible terms.

The Bible

We search the world for truth. We cull
The good, the true, the beautiful,
From graven stone and written scroll,
And all old flower fields of the soul;
And, weary seekers of the best,
We come back laden from our quest,
To find that all the sages said
Is in the Book our mothers read.

—John Greenleaf Whittier

Structure Within The Paragraph

Observation correctly relates terms.

Terms are used in a given structure—phrases, clauses, sentences—within each paragraph and paragraphs in segments to clarify their meaning.

The words of the LORD are pure words: as silver tried in a furnace of earth, purified seven times.

Psalm 12:6

Chapter 4

Structure Within The Paragraph

The next step is the observation of relations and interrelations between terms. However we must first see what is meant by *structure*.

1. Definition of Structure

(1) *General Structure* — This involves *all* of the relations and interrelations which bind terms into a literary unit.

(2) *Restricted Structure* — This is used to denote the framework or skeleton of a passage. It denotes the most essential terms and their relations with each other.

Note: This study will concentrate primarily upon the *Restricted Structure* or "*core*" of the passage. Although we will not entirely ignore the *General Structure,* only a little attention will be given to it, and that only incidentally.

It is very easy to become bogged down in the study of the Bible, because of the very complex grammatical structure of many Bible passages. We become bogged down when we follow the details of the "sidepaths" prematurely. It is very important that we give first consideration to the "*core*" of the passage *(Restricted Structure)* before proceeding on into the details. By "*core*" of the passage, we mean the main "stream of thought" as it flows through that passage. This will be covered in more detail later.

2. Units of Structure

We should be able to recognize each of these in a Bible passage.

(1) The *Phrase* — Grammar: A group of two or more associated words, not containing a subject and predicate. One example is the prepositional phrase.

(2) The *Clause* — Grammar: A group of terms, including a subject and predicate, and sometimes one or more phrases, constituting a partial (or whole) unit of thought and expression.

(3) The *Sentence* — Grammar: A group of words containing subject and predicate. There are declarative, interrogative, imperative, and exclamatory sentences, or a single word, in the case of the simple imperative. A sentence must contain a complete thought.

(4) The *Paragraph* — Grammer: A group of sentences constituting a unit of thought and expression. The paragraph develops a point or subject. In modern English the paragraph is much more clearly defined than it is in the Bible.

(5) A *Segment* — In Bible study it is a group of paragraphs constituting a unit of thought, or developing a thought.

Illustration: In my study of Paul's Epistle to the Romans I have one *division* entitled "Dispensational." The *segments* under that are as follows:

> 3. *Dispensational* — *9:1 – 11:36*
>
> > *(1) Israel's past*   *9:1–33*
> >
> > *(2) Israel's present*   *10:1–21*
> >
> > *(3) Israel's future*   *11:1–36*

Each of the 3 points above indicate *segments* of that division. [See next point for the *divisions.*]

(6) A *Division* — In Bible study, some books have *divisions*. This is a group of segments constituting a larger unit of thought or subject matter.

Illustration: In my study of Romans, I have divided the book as follows:

> *-1.Introduction*   *1:1–17*
>
> *-2.Doctrinal*   *1:18 – 8:39*
>
> *-3.Dispensational* *9:1 – 11:36*

-4. Practical   *12:1 – 15:13*

-5. Conclusion   *15:14 – 16:27*

Each of the 5 parts shown above would be a division of the book

(7) The *Book* — This is a Bible division. The Bible contains 66 books in all, each of them written for a specific purpose at a given time. Some are history, some are prophecy, some are for instruction, some are poetry. Each book of the Bible has its own characteristics.

3. Importance of Structure

If the Bible student is to find Bible passages unfolding before his or her very eyes, they must become *structure conscious*. And by that, we are not speaking of cold, mechanical grammatical analysis. That is what Israel was doing in a sense in Isaiah's time (Isaiah 28:10, 13 - *"For precept must be upon precept, precept upon precept; line upon line, line upon line; here a little, and there a little:...But the word of the LORD was unto them precept upon precept, precept upon precept; line upon line, line upon line; here a little, and there a little; that they might go, and fall backward, and be broken, and snared, and taken."*).

However, to miss the structure of a passage is to miss the essential message of that passage. We must know what the action is, who are the actors, and the effects of that action. We need to know the "stream of thought" of the passage under our consideration before we can understand the passage well. If we are to *live* and *teach* the passage we must know it well.

4. Types of Structure

(1) As to *apparency*: The *obvious* and the *latent* (surface and subsurface).

The *surface* or *obvious:* There are some elements of structure which are evident, explicit and readily apparent to the observer. Examples of these would be such passages as Galatians 5:22–23 and Proverbs 6:16–19.

Subsurface or *latent:* Those structural elements which are hidden, elusive, and implicit. These are not readily observable, and thus are called *subsurface*. Many examples of this can be given, for one, the word "vain" in 1 Corinthians 15, where the chapter might be titled, "Is our Gospel vain?"

Note: These distinctions have nothing to do with the importance or the depth of spiritual significance of that part of the passage. They simply speak of whether or not the truth is easily seen, and thus *apparent* to the observer. Through these distinctions we separate that which is obvious to the eye and the mind from that which may be discovered only by a more careful and detailed study. *All* of the Bible is important, and we *must not* neglect the hidden, or *subsurface,* truths.

(2) As to *importance:* The *primary* and the *subordinate (secondary).* "Many misleading interpretations have been made because that which was intended to be subordinate has been identified wrongly as primary." [1]

Note: Again, this has nothing whatsoever to do with the relative importance of the truths taught, excepting as they may be misunderstood. It has to do with the structural relations of the passage being studied. You see, each passage has one primary truth being presented. Then, in addition, some passages may give us one or more subordinate truths. Every teaching of the Bible is important, and we do not minimize that fact.

5. Methods of Analyzing Structure

Method is simply orderly procedure. In this course it is presented as the *means* of arriving at an understanding of what the Bible *says* so that we may discover what it *means.*

(1) Sentences in the Bible

There are three things we should know about the sentences of the Bible:

-1. Sentences in the Bible are, for the most part, similar to sentences in other types of literature in that they follow rules of grammar.

-2. However, Bible sentences also differ in many ways from sentences in other literature. This will be obvious to the student.

   The sentences of the Bible are not so clearly defined as those in other literature. This is especially true of the New Testament Epistles.

-3. We need to understand that the original writings of the Scriptures had no chapter or verse divisions. There was also no punctuation. In fact, there was no spacing between the words in the original Greek of the New Testament. The sentence structure of the original is such that, in many cases, the sentence may ramble on and on. Other sentences may be very clearly defined.

Before we become too critical of the original writers and their works, before we consider them to be backward and uneducated, we must realize that the Bible was written in another culture and at another time. It is a historical fact that languages are in a process of constant change. This also includes punctuation and sentence structure, as well as vocabulary. These things have changed just in my own lifetime.

Also, God did not design the Scriptures to be translated *only* into modern English. If we were able to speak all of the multiplied scores of languages spoken on earth, and into which the Scriptures have been translated, we would "take off our shoes" in awe and reverence at the great wisdom of our Almighty, All-wise God in making it just as it was written in those original writings. To judge the Bible by our own limited knowledge of language is to be very foolish.

(2) Essential parts of the sentence

These are *subject* and *predicate*. That is, something to talk about, and something to say about it.

This will be review for most people. But before going on to the next step of observation, we must be sure that our minds are all refreshed in these areas of knowledge.

-1. *Subject*: This is a word or group of words which name the person or thing about whom or which the statement is made. In its simplest form, it consists of a noun or a pronoun.

-2. *Predicate*: This is a word or a group of words which make a statement about the subject. In its simplest form, it consists of a verb alone. This is the action part of the sentence. It always contains a verb. The object is part of the predicate. The direct and indirect objects are the result of an action and work with action verbs. The predicate nominative is a state of being denoted by the being verbs.

-3. *Object*: (direct, indirect, or predicate nominative): The direct and indirect objects are the result of an action and work with action verbs. The predicate nominative is a state of being verb denoted by the being verbs.

The simple subject and the simple predicate may both have modifiers and other accessories. These other accessories may be adjectives, which modify a noun or a pronoun; or adverbs, which modify a verb, an adjective, or another adverb.

(3) The sentence

In order for a group of words to be a sentence it must make a statement. That statement must be made about a person, place, or a thing, called its *subject*. There are three things, all beginning with the letter "s," which must be true of every sentence: *subject*, *statement*, and *sense*.

Which of the following are sentences?

When he was a very young lad.

Because he was sensitive and shy.

Reading the London periodicals found in his foster father's business house. Also the works of Moore, Byron, and Goldsmith.

The beautiful garden which Edgar loved more than anything else.

The sweet-scented vines creeping over the garden wall.

I think you will have to agree that none of these is a sentence, because none of them makes sense.

Now, making sentences of some of the above we see the following:

When he was a very young lad, Edgar Allan Poe accompanied his foster parents to England.

He was frequently misunderstood, because he was sensitive and shy.

He loved to read the poems of Keats and Burns, also the works of Moore, Byron, and Wordsworth.

He also loved the sweet-scented vines creeping over the old garden wall.

We must know the following facts if we are to be able to recognize a sentence:

-1. In order to be a sentence, a group of words must contain a subject and a predicate, which are words that tell you *who is something, or what does something.*

-2. You can always correct your own errors in selecting subject and predicate by reading the two together, just as you would read a sentence, to see if they make sense.

Example: From the sentence, "*First, I thank my God through Jesus Christ for you all, that your faith is spoken of throughout the whole world,*" we pick the subject and the predicate. The subject is "*I,*" and the predicate is "*thank.*" Read them together, "*I thank.*" Does that make sense? Yes it does.

-3. The predicate consists of a *does–* or *is–*word and any other words going with it to complete the sense.

-4. The subject consists of the word or group of words telling what or who does or is something.

(4) The Subject Part and the Predicate Part

The *Subject Part:* All of the words belonging to the subject will be called the *subject part* in the exercises to follow.

The *Predicate Part:* All of the words belonging to the predicate will be called the *predicate part.*

Thus, all of the words in any sentence will belong to one part or the other. This fact should help to simplify our analysis of any Bible sentence.

Examples of this:

— *Natural Order* –

Subject Part	Predicate Part
1. Thomas Jefferson	lived at Monticello, Virginia.
2. He	loved to study languages.

— *Inverted Order* –

Predicate Part	*Subject Part*
1. Down crashed	the great airplane.
2. Away ran	the startled deer.
3. Home from his wanderings came at last	the weary exile.

Sentences from our King James Bible are not always quite so simple as the above illustrations. We will attempt to give some illustrations of Bible sentences in the following, all from Philippians. Punctuation will be ignored in some of these. Notice, the single underline is *subject,* the bold is *predicate.*

1:3   <u>I</u> **thank** my God upon every remembrance of you.

1:9   And this <u>I</u> **pray**, that your <u>love</u> **may abound** yet more and more in knowledge and in all judgment.

1:21   For to me <u>to live</u> **is** Christ, and <u>to die</u> **is** gain.
       ["to live" and "to die" are infinitives, here used as subjects]

1:15   <u>Some</u> indeed **preach** Christ even of envy and strife; and some also of good will.

2:5   (<u>You</u>) **Let** this mind **be** in you, which was also in Christ Jesus.

(5) Parts of Speech

You are encouraged to consult a grammar book if you do not remember or have never mastered these parts of speech.

-1. *Nouns* – the name of something as a person, place, thing or idea: as *tree, boy, health, happiness.*

There are 3 classifications of *nouns:*

1)   Common noun

2)   Proper noun

3)   Collective noun

-2. *Pronoun* – a word used for a noun. The noun to which a pronoun refers is called its antecedent.

There are 5 classifications of *pronouns:*

1)   Personal pronouns — *I, you, he, she, it*

2)   Relative pronouns — *who, which, that, what, whatsoever, whichever, whichsoever*

       3)   Interrogative pronouns — *who, which, what*

       4)   Demonstrative pronouns — *this, that, these, those*

       5)   Indefinite pronouns — *some, somebody, each, everyone, any, anyone, one*

-3. *Adjective* – They modify a noun or a pronoun.

-4. *Verb* – These make a statement about the subject of the sentence or clause. There are two kinds of verbs one that expresses action, and the other is a being verb. There are many classifications and properties of verbs. These can be found in a grammar text.

-5. *Adverb* – This is a word which modifies a verb, an adjective, or another adverb.

-6. *Preposition* – This is a connecting word used to show the relation of a noun or a pronoun to some other word in the sentence: as, *to, from, for, below, against.*

-7. *Conjunction* – This is a connecting word used to join words or groups of words in a sentence: as, *and, or, while, if, as.*

-8. *Interjection* – This is an exclamatory word which has little or no grammatical relation to the rest of the sentence: **What!?**

---

[1] *Independent Bible Study,* by Irving Jensen, p. 51.

Exercise

1. Work on the following passages and pick out the simple subject and the simple predicate.

      Phil.   1:24

                  1:29

                  2:10

                  2:12

                  2:14

                  3:1

                  3:7

                  3:13

                  4:6

                  4:9

2. In the following passages pick out the "subject part" and the "predicate part." *(Not every word needs to be included in all of them, as some have many subordinate clauses.)*

   Phil.   1:12

           1:19

           2:20

           2:26

           2:29

           3:14

           3:17

           3:20

           4:2

           4:16

Study Questions

1. Distinguish between *general structure* and *restricted structure*.

2. If we involve ourselves first in the *restricted structure* what problems do we avoid?

3. We have given 7 different units of structure. What are they? Describe each.

4. What are the types of structure *as to apparency?*

5. What are the types of structure *as to importance?*

6. How are sentences in the Bible similar, and how are they different from the sentences found in other literature in the English language?

7. Why should we not be critical about the Bible, its punctuation, its vocabulary, and the nature of its sentences?

8. What are the *essential parts* of the sentence? Please explain each of these.

9. What 3 things, all beginning with an "s," must be true before a group of words is a sentence?

10. Before a group of words can be a sentence what must be true? (See page 62)

11. Name the parts of speech and tell what each is.
    [If you cannot identify these, please consult an English grammar textbook.]

Understand?

Many things in the Bible I cannot understand; many things in the Bible I only think I understand; but there are many things in the Bible I cannot MISunderstand.

—*Author unknown*

The Core of the Structure

Observation finds the core or main "Stream Of Thought" of the passage.

Identifying the core thought which is the main "Stream of Thought" of the passage enables us to connect the truth of each passage to all Scripture.

All scripture is given by inspiration of God, and is profitable for doctrine, for reproof, for correction, for instruction in righteousness: [17]That the man of God may be perfect, throughly furnished unto all good works.

2 Timothy 3:16–17

Chapter 5

The Core of the Structure

We have discussed the *terms,* and the structure of the *sentences.* What I will be presenting in this chapter is one of the most interesting and helpful methods for analyzing a sentence of Scripture that I have found.

The *core is* the "stream of thought" of the passage. This is often missed by the student when they study an extended sentence in the Scriptures, where there are many modifying words, phrases, and clauses. It is also missed frequently in even shorter Bible sentences, due to the carelessness of the observer.

There are a number of ways of showing the *core* of a passage by using diagrams. Since we study best with a pencil in hand (and in use), the samples on the following pages will give us an idea of *some* of the ways in which we can use that pencil effectively. Notice, I did not say "pen." The use of diagrams helps us to clear away the "foliage" so we may see the "trunk" of the "tree" of Truth. The real pleasure in this comes when we see the real message by separating the primary from the subordinate.

Remember, we are looking for the main "stream of thought." We must search out carefully the principal subject, the main verbal action, and the results or object of that action.

We may ask the following questions:
(1) What is the passage talking about (noun)?
(2) What action is taking place (predicate or verb)?
(3) What are the results of that action, or who/what is the object of that action?

The pages which follow will demonstrate various kinds of diagrams which may be used to show the *core* of the sentence in Scripture. Let me constantly remind you that diagrams are the means to an end and not the end. The end is knowledge of the Scripture. To lose oneself in the making of diagrams is to miss the entire point. It would be to fall into one of the devil's traps.

How We Should Use a Pencil

Let me also talk to you about the use of a pencil. We need to use both the pencil and *scratch* paper. We should jot down the ideas that occur to us as we read and study. Though, we should not regard the first thing that we think of and write down as being final.

Years ago I made some notes as I read through the Psalms. I still have that little spiral notebook. It humbles me, for it shows me just how little I knew about the Word of God at that time. Many of my observations were far off. Of course, part of the reason was that I did not yet have a definite method of Bible study in which I considered the terms first, then the sentences, etc. However, it is a good idea to jot down every idea, and make every sketch that occurs to you.

This look at the *core* of the sentences will help you to have an idea of just how to work with the pencil. Use it freely. Don't stop writing and rewriting until you are sure that you have arrived at the proper conclusion. You may come back in later years and revise your notes.

The following three pages contain examples of various types of *core* diagrams.

EXAMPLE No. 1

– STRUCTURAL DIAGRAM –
(Capital letters indicate the *core*.)

– Hebrews 1:1–3

GOD,   Who at sundry times and in divers
manners spake in time past unto
the fathers by the prophets,

HATH   in these last days

SPOKEN   UNTO US

        BY HIS SON Whom He hath appointed Heir of
all things,
by Whom also He made the worlds;

     WHO being the brightness of His glory
and the express image of His
Person, and upholding all things
by the
Word of His power,
when He had by Himself
purged our sins,

SAT DOWN on the right hand of the
Majesty on High;

This *core* says:

"GOD HATH SPOKEN UNTO US BY HIS SON WHO SAT DOWN."

- The core in this passage remains as stated, but we can see from the clauses in this passage the comparison of the Old and New Testaments.

GOD

"spake"	"Hath spoken"
"unto the fathers"	"unto us"
"by the prophets"	"by His Son"
"at sundry times and in divers manners"	"WHO SAT DOWN"
(Past and continuous Revelation)	(Completed Revelation)
OLD TESTAMENT	NEW TESTAMENT [1]

EXAMPLE No. 2

– I Peter 1:2 (in part)

This diagram is slightly different, in that it is not a complete sentence.

ELECT	according to the foreknowledge of *God, the Father*
THROUGH SANCTIFICATION	of the *Spirit*
UNTO	
OBEDIENCE AND SPRINKLING	of the blood of *Jesus Christ*

Note: See how the Trinity plays a part in this passage. Each person of the Godhead is seen to be active in our Divine Election.

Note: Remember, a passage of Scripture says only one thing. We cannot make it say other than what it says in fact. However, we may exercise some liberty in showing the *core* of the passage. There is only one *core*; it is rarely ever a matter of opinion. Yet, it may be demonstrated in various ways.

– Philippians 1:29–30 (in part)

IT   not only
                                    TO BELIEVE on Him
                                but also
                                    TO SUFFER for His sake.

IS
GIVEN
            UNTO
            YOU   Having the same conflict which ye
                         saw in me, and now hear to be in me.

OR, more clearly:

not only
            TO BELIEVE   on Him

but also
            TO SUFFER   for His sake

IS
GIVEN
            UNTO
            YOU

The Syntactical Display

The Unifying Theme of the Paragraph

The principal feature of a paragraph is a unifying theme. Analyzing how the supporting statements of the paragraph are related to one another is probably the hardest task for the Bible Student. There are occasional independent sentences which are hard to relate to the theme of the paragraph. But apart from these, the student will be dealing most often with relating clauses and phrases within each sentence.

A way of analyzing a passage is by means of what is called *the Syntactical Display.* By *syntax* is meant "the arrangement and interrelationship of words in phrases and sentences." The *Syntactical Display* works especially well on an extended passage.

We must realize that every word in a passage is affected to some degree by the following:

(1) It is affected by its grammatical function in the phrase, clause, or sentence. That would be noun, verb, adjective, adverb, etc.

(2) It is affected by the words, phrases, clauses, sentences, and paragraphs which surround it. This has to do with the immediate context first of all. The student must learn to distinguish the main assertions from supporting assertions in the passage.

The Clause

We explained that the *clause* is a group of words which has a subject and a verb/predicate and which forms part of a sentence. *Clauses* may be classified under two categories:

(1) **type of *clause***

(2) **grammatical function of the *clause*.**

Recognizing Types of Clauses

There are three types of **clauses**.

(1) The *independent clause:* It is the main or principal clause (i.e., any clause that expresses a complete idea and that can stand alone).

(2) The *coordinate clause:* It is any clause that forms one part of a compound sentence.

(3) The *dependent* or *subordinate clause:* This is any clause which does not express a complete thought and which cannot stand alone.

We must not only be able to recognize these various types of **clauses**, but we must be alert to some of the words used to introduce them. The following list is given for your study:

(1) Coordinating conjunctions: *and, or, nor, for, but, neither ... nor, either ... or, both ... and, not only ... but also*

(2) Adversative coordinating conjunctions: *but, except*

(3) Emphatic coordinating conjunctives: *yea, certainly, in fact*

(4) Inferential coordinating conjunctives: *therefore, then, wherefore, so*

(5) Transitional coordinating conjunctives: *and, moreover, then*

(6) Subordinating conjunctions: *when, because, if, since, although, that, where*

(7) Subordinating relative pronouns: *who, whose, whom, which, that* [2]

Considering the Grammatical Function of the Clause

The following are the three functions of the *clause* which must be especially recognized by the Bible student:

(1) The *noun clause* is any clause that functions as a noun. Noun clauses may function (a) nominatively — an example of this, *"That Tom had quit* was told his boss." [Not many examples of the nominative use are found in the Bible.]   (b) accusatively — "And GOD saw *that the wickedness of man was great in the earth ...*" (Gen. 6:5); and (c) appositionally — "... behold, if it be truth, and the things certain, *that such abomination is wrought among you*" (Deut. 13:14).

(2) The *relative clause* performs the same function as an adjective by modifying or qualifying a noun.

(3) The *adverbial clause* functions as an adverb and modifies or qualifies a verb, adjective, adverb, or prepositional phrase. The main types of these are (a) circumstantial ("while ..."), (b) temporal [having to do with time] ("when ..."), (c) conditional ("if ..."), (d) purpose ("in order that ..."), (e) result ("so ... that"), (f) concessive ("although ...," "even though ..."), (g) causal ("because ..."), and (h) restrictive ("only ..." "if ... not ...").

The Phrase

The *phrase* was defined as a group of related words without a subject and a predicate. There are three basic types of *phrases:*

(1) *Prepositional:* This is a group of words, lacking a verb, which are introduced by a preposition. "I say unto thee, Arise, and take up thy bed, and go thy way *into* thine house" (Mark 2:11). "Into" is the preposition, and "house" is the object of the preposition. "Thine" modifies or qualifies "house."

(2) *Participial:* This is a group of words introduced by a verb form acting as an adjective. "The boy *resting* in the shade was tired. "Resting" is the participle. Notice how it modifies the noun "boy."

(3) The *infinitive phrase* is a group of words introduced by the word "to" followed immediately by a verb. "Whether is it easier *to say* to the sick of the palsy, Thy sins be forgiven thee …" (Mark 2:9). The words "to say" are the infinitive.

Infinitive phrases may be (a) adverbial, doing the work of an adverb, modifying verbs, etc. "I came not *to call* the righteous …" (Mark 2:17). It modifies "came." (b) Adjectival, doing the work of an adjective, modifying nouns, etc. "But that ye may know that the Son of man hath power on earth *to forgive* sins" (Mark 2:10). "Power" is a noun, and "to forgive" modifies or qualifies it, telling about that power. (c) Nominal, serving the function of a noun. A classic illustration, "For to me *to live* is Christ, and *to die* is gain" (Phil. 1:21). The infinitives here serve as subjects of the sentence, as we have seen in an earlier exercise.

Understanding the Syntactical Display

Below are some samples of the *Syntactical Display*. This display shows the interrelationship of the words, phrases, and sentences in the passage. Notice how to understand these diagrams:

(1) Each statement, clause, and phrase is written out in the *natural order* of the text. Thus, one can copy the passage from their Bible as it appears.

(2) Each unit is isolated on a separate line. As you copy, divide the passage into its various parts. You will see this in the examples given.

(3) The theme statement (or proposition) is brought out to the left-hand margin. This is the main statement of the passage. There may be parallels to that theme which are also brought out to the left.

(4) Those parts which modify or qualify the theme proposition are slightly indented. Notice in the first example, the first line is a subordinate statement to the theme statement, "we beseech you, and exhort you."

(5) Material which modifies or qualifies the subordinate units which are subordinate to the theme statement are indented one step further and so on. Notice how we move to the right each time a subordinate unit occurs.

(6) By drawing arrows immediately to the left of all subordinate units we indicate the elements to which these modifying units are linked.

One should understand the basics of grammar sufficiently well to be able to note which are the main or theme statements, and which are subordinate.

Note: As we have repeated over and over, such a diagram as this must not be the purpose, or end, of the study. It must be the means to the end of understanding the main thrust and the sense of any given passage. In my own experience, I have very rarely resorted to such a diagram as this. Most passages are not too difficult to understand. Though, I encourage you to do a *Syntactical Display* once in a while. You will enjoy the challenge, and it will teach you a great deal about the passage itself.

On the following pages are some examples of *Syntactical Display*. You should study each of them over carefully. Be sure that you understand the purpose of every part.

---

[1] Adapted from *Independent Bible Study,* by Irving Jensen, Moody Bible Institute, 1963, pages 53-54.

Mr. Jensen does not follow the King James Version. His charts are quite involved. It is easy to be so taken by the method that we fail to realize the aim of the study.

[2] Adapted from *Toward an Exegetical Theology,* by Kaiser, pages 96–97.

– I Thessalonians 4:1–8

1.   Furthermore then ... brethren

we beseech you,
    and
exhort you by the Lord Jesus,
    that as ye have received
         of us
         how ye ought to walk
           and
         to please God,
so ye would abound more and more.

2.   For ye know what commandments we gave you
         by the Lord Jesus

3.   For this is { the will of God, even
         your sanctification

that ye should abstain from fornication:

4.   That every one of you should know how to possess his vessel
    in sanctification
     and
    honour;

5.   Not in the lust of concupiscence
    even as the Gentiles
        which know not God

6.   that no man go beyond
     and } his brother
    defraud

    in any matter:
because that the Lord is the
    avenger of all such
      as we have forewarned you
       and
      testified.

7.   For God hath not called us
    unto uncleanness
    but unto holiness,

8.   He therefore that despiseth { despiseth not
        man but God

Who hath also given unto us
His Holy Spirit.

– Ephesians 5:15–21

15. See then that ye walk circumspectly,
       not as fools
       but as wise

16. Redeeming the time
          because the days are evil

   17. Wherefore
      be ye not unwise,
      but understanding what the will of the Lord is.

      18. And be not drunk with wine,
                    wherein is excess;
      but be filled with the Spirit;

             19. Speaking to yourselves
                  in psalms
                     and
                  hymns
                     and
                  spiritual songs

     singing
        and   } in your heart to the Lord
     making melody

             20. Giving thanks
                  always
                  for all things
                  unto God and the Father
                  in the Name of our Lord Jesus Christ

             21. Submitting yourselves
                  one to another
                  in the fear of God.

A Conclusion: *How to live wisely* — Eph. 5:15–21

1. Redeem the time (5:16)

2. Understand the will of God (5:17)

3. Be filled with the Holy Spirit (5:18–21)

    — EVIDENCED BY:

      (1) By spiritual conversation (5:19a)

      (2) By spiritual songs (5:19b)

      (3) By continual thanksgiving (5:20)

      (4) By submitting one to another (5:21)

Exercise

(Use this page and the next two pages for this exercise.)

1. Make a *core* diagram or *syntactical display* of Romans 1:1–7. [Keep it as simple as possible.]

2. Follow "*the mystery*" in Ephesians 3:1–12. Use a *core* diagram, a *syntactical display,* or possibly a *summary* of everything Paul says about this subject in this passage.

Work Sheet

Work Sheet

Work Sheet

Study Questions

1. Define the *core* of the passage.

2. How may we find the *main stream of thought* of the passage?

3. What three questions may we ask?

4. Describe the use of a pencil as we study the Bible.

5. How many *cores* are there in a passage?

6. How much liberty may we use in expressing the *core* of a passage?

7. What is the principal feature of a paragraph?

8. What is a clause?

9. What are the three types of clauses and how do we recognize each?

10. What is a phrase?

11. What are the three types of phrases and how do we recognize each?

12. Explain the indentation in the *Syntactical Display*.

Within this ample volume lies
The mystery of mysteries.
Happiest they of human race
To whom God has given grace
To read, to fear, to hope, to pray,
To lift the latch, to force the way;
And better had they ne'er been born
That read to doubt or read to scorn.

— Sir Walter Scott

Developing a Broader View

Observation finds the "Main Truth."

Connecting the "Stream of Thought" in each passage helps us identify the "Main Thought" in each paragraph/chapter.

Knowing this first, that no prophecy of the scripture is of any private interpretation. [21]For the prophecy came not in old time by the will of man: but holy men of God spake as they were moved by the Holy Ghost.

2 Peter 1:20–21

Chapter 6

Developing a Broader View

At this point we begin to build upon what we have learned so far about the terms of Scripture, and about the study of the sentences of the Bible. We are beginning a study of the analysis of the paragraphs of the Bible. Again we say, the approach here is basic to *all* systems and methods of Bible Study, in that a familiarity with the contents of the paragraphs and sentences is basic to everything else.

It is necessary for the Bible student to begin to consider the Bible by paragraphs, rather than by chapter and verse only. The Scriptures, as originally written, had no chapter or verse divisions. These are of more or less recent origin (chapter divisions having been devised in the early 13th Century and verse divisions about 1551).

However, we must not think that chapter and verse designations are unimportant to us. They are very important. How else would we be able to indicate a specific part of a paragraph by way of reference? And how else could we find that indicated part in the Bible? Consider the dilemma if only paragraphs had been numbered, rather than the chapters and verses, as we find them. The numbered passages would necessarily be long, and consequently, we would have great difficulty in determining the specific thoughts (words and phrases) needed. In turning, for example, to "Romans, paragraph 6" (wherever that might be), we would have to search through many sentences, and still would not be sure just which specific part would be the one needed for our reference and study. Also, consider the difficulty of memorizing Scripture by lengthy paragraphs rather than by shorter verses. What a confusing task that would be!

Coming back to our thought, it is very important that we carefully avoid the habit of treating each verse as if it were a separate paragraph. Each verse is not a paragraph in itself, and it is also frequently true that a verse is not even a complete sentence.

One important means of studying the entire context is to purposely study a book of the Bible by paragraphs. In order to do this, the paragraph divisions must first be determined. After that, the main idea ("main truth") of the paragraph is found. Then the paragraph may be outlined, or key sentences may be chosen – these are sentences which express the central theme of the paragraph. A sheet is included in the Appendix on which the paragraphs have been designated for each chapter of Paul's Epistle to the Philippians. This will be used as a guide for our paragraph study.

Paragraph Divisions

Some Bibles have the paragraph divisions indicated with a pilcrow (¶), while a large number of Bible editions do not. A word of caution: The divisions in the Scofield Reference Edition of the Bible *do not* always follow the paragraphs. For an illustration of this, see Philippians 2:12–30 in the 1917 edition of the Scofield Reference Bible. (We do not recommend the 1967 edition, *New Scofield Reference Bible,* as it follows the Nestlé Greek text.)

Various Bibles differ in their paragraph divisions, the main differences being due to how finely the passage is divided. Some divide the subject matter into much smaller units of thought, and for that reason, have more paragraphs than others.

Whatever manner you follow in determining the paragraph divisions, you need to carefully analyze the passage in order to assure yourself that the divisions are correct. Then you must determine the subject of the paragraph.

The Main Truth

Every paragraph will have a main idea, or "main truth," as we will call it in this study. The contents of any chosen paragraph must present that "main truth," or it is not a paragraph. The "main truth" is the subject or main idea.

The idea is to search out the "main truth," and write it in the form of a title, a phrase, or a simple sentence. Compound sentences or phrases are thus ruled out, for they indicate more than one idea rather than a single main idea.

The "main truth" is not determined in a few moments, it often takes careful analysis, prayerful meditation, and study. It is important that you read the paragraph repeatedly. Sometimes it will help if you summarize the contents of the paragraph. We may find that what we have chosen is not a paragraph. It may be two or more paragraphs, or it may be only a part of a paragraph. Our careful search for the "main truth" will help us to check up on our paragraph divisions.

We must search the paragraph carefully to determine what is that main idea, or "main truth." Remember, use a pencil first. It is not easy to erase work done with a pen.

Assignment

Use the "Main Truth Summary" form found on pages 99 and 101. Use only helps necessary for word studies. See the example of the "Main Truths Summary" (or "Bible Study Worksheet") on pages 153 and 154.

1. Check to see if the paragraph divisions are correct. Make any necessary corrections.

2. Do word studies and core diagrams as you work on each paragraph. You should research *at least* ten words from each chapter. Focus especially on verbs and nouns. See page 127. Write out the meaning. Do this on a separate sheet of paper and have it ready to turn in with your Main Truth Summaries. Be sure to follow the guidelines for *non-routine terms* found on pages 42 and 43.

3. Find the "main truth" of each paragraph in the chapter. Use scratch paper to begin this and then move it to the "Main Truth Summary" Sheet. These can be written as a *title*, a *phrase*, or a *simple sentence*.

Note: Later, as you become familiar with the method, and as you become better acquainted with the book of Philippians, you may wish to revise your "main truth" summaries. A second sheet is also provided for this purpose on page 101. If you are taking this course in a class setting, you may continue making revisions up until the final session, when you will turn your summaries in to the instructor.

4. Later, when all of the "main truths" have been determined, try to discover the primary subject of the chapter ("chapter title"). This also requires much careful study and prayerful thought.

5. Finally, find the "theme" of the entire book.

Most books of the Bible follow a clear and distinct theme throughout. Do not be surprised, though, if your own idea of the theme of a specific book changes over the years as you study it over and over again. You should be able to come up with a pretty good idea of the main teaching of the book by following the plan set forth here: paragraphs first, chapters second, then the book.

Later on, after you have studied the book more carefully, and as each individual section is discussed in class, you may wish to revise your original conclusions about the chapters and the book as a whole. Revisions are a part of study, do not hesitate to make them when necessary.

However, please do your own work. If you copy the summaries of your fellow students during class discussion, and you may do so, please do not use their work in drawing your own conclusions.

Work Sheet

Work Sheet

Work Sheet

Work Sheet

WORK SHEET

Turn this sheet in.

MAIN TRUTH SUMMARY

PHILIPPIANS

	CHAPTER 1	CHAPTER 2	CHAPTER 3	CHAPTER 4
Chapter Title				
Main Truths of the Paragraphs	1:1–2	2:1–11	3:1–3	4:1
	1:3–11		3:4–6	4:2–3
	1:12–18	2:12–18	3:7–14	4:4–7
	1:19–26	2:19–30	3:15–16	4:8–9
	1:27–30		3:17–21	4:10–20
				4:21–22
				4:23

SECOND WORK SHEET

To turn in your revisions.

MAIN TRUTH SUMMARY   PHILIPPIANS

	CHAPTER 1	CHAPTER 2	CHAPTER 3	CHAPTER 4
Chapter Title				
Main Truths of the Paragraphs	1:1–2	2:1–11	3:1–3	4:1
	1:3–11	2:12–18	3:4–6	4:2–3
	1:12–18		3:7–14	4:4–7
	1:19–26	2:19–30	3:15–16	4:8–9
	1:27–30		3:17–21	4:10–20
				4:21–22
				4:23

"Faith Focused"

I suppose that if all the time I have prayed for faith were put together, it would amount to months. I used to say, "What we want is faith; if we only have faith, we can turn Chicago upside down, or rather right side up." I thought that someday faith would come down and strike me like lightning. But faith did not seem to come. One day I read in the tenth chapter of Romans, "Now, faith cometh by hearing, and hearing by the Word of God." I closed my Bible and prayed for faith. I opened my Bible and began to study, and faith has been growing ever since.

—*D. L. Moody*

Bible Book Studies

Part 1

Getting the Background of the Bible Book

Observation studies the Background of the Book.

All the information gathered from our study of terms, core truths, and main thoughts must also be understood in the culture and setting of the time in which it was given.

One of themselves, even a prophet of their own, said, The Cretians are alway liars, evil beasts, slow bellies.

Titus 1:12

Chapter 7

Bible Book Studies

Part 1

Getting the Background of the Bible Book

When one makes a study of any book of the Bible, in order to be careful and thorough, that student must make a serious effort to know the background facts behind the book. The student must first make a thorough study of the Scriptures themselves. After that, there are any number of sources which can be of great help in determining the background of any book.

The following six facts must be determined:

1. **The historical period.** The political rulers, empires, wars, conditions, etc. A chart prepared by the student is helpful here. This study could require much research, but it is time well spent, especially if you will record your findings on a chart in such a way that it will be helpful to you in future studies of other books written during the same times.

2. **The time.** When was the book written?

   (1) Give references from the book which reveal specific points of time (if they can be found in that book). Also, it is helpful if you reference other books which cast light on the times and the conditions existing in those times.

(2) Locate the time of writing the book with reference to the lifespan of the writer. A chart also may be used to great advantage in this.

3. **The writer.** Learn all you can about him, his personality, his past, his work. Make biographical notes as you read. There will be more on biographical studies later.

4. **Place of writing.** To what place was the book addressed? Where was the writer when he wrote it? What were his conditions? Determine these things as much as possible from a study of the book itself before turning to other helps.

5. **Recipients.** To whom was the book written? What was their location, and their history? Again, try to get the facts from the book itself, then from related books, then from helps. A knowledge of geography and history is invaluable here.

In the case of an Epistle to a Church, study the founding of that Church, then follow that with a look at the visits made by the Apostle to that Church. An Epistle to an individual requires that you find all you can about that person. Again we say, use helps last.

6. **Purpose.** What problems in their lives made the book necessary? Again, search this out in the book before turning to the commentaries and other helps. You will be glad that you made a firsthand study — besides, the commentaries are not always correct, and some of their errors are flagrant. You need to learn to do your own studying.

Some Helps You Can Use

Among these are the following: A Bible encyclopedia, a standard encyclopedia, a Bible dictionary, and a Bible Handbook. It is helpful to consult books which cover the history of the periods of time in question. A good knowledge of geography is invaluable. Commentaries can sometimes help with this. However, remember that the works of man are not always dependable. We have often found traditional views, rather than Biblical truths, presented in dictionaries, etc.

In general, whatever you can learn which will help you to understand the six background facts given will be helpful to you in understanding the book.

**Light obeyed increaseth light,
Light rejected bringeth night.**

Assignment

Do a background study of the book of Philippians.

1. Make sure to learn all that you can from the book of Philippians itself.

2. Find out all that you can about the city of Philippi and the founding of the Church in that city. Use the book of Acts for this.

3. Look at some of the people mentioned in the Epistle, and, using a concordance, find their names in other books. This may help you.

4. Now, give all that you can for each of the 6 background facts as listed above.

   If you are taking this in a class setting have your assignment ready to be turned in to your instructor at the next class session.

Work Sheet

Work Sheet

Work Sheet

Work Sheet

Work Sheet

Work Sheet

God's Word

Last eve I paused beside a blacksmith's door
And heard the anvil ring the vesper chime;
Then looking in, I saw upon the floor
Old hammers worn with beating years of time.

How many anvils have you had, said I,
To wear and batter all these hammers so?
Just one, he answered, then with twinkling eye,
The anvil wears the hammers out, you know.

And so, I thought, the anvil of God's Word
For ages skeptic blows have beat upon;
Yet though the noise of falling blows were heard,
The anvil is unworn—the hammers gone.

—*John Clifford, D.D.*

Bible Book Studies

Part 2

Biographical Studies

Observation makes Biographical Studies.

Do Biographical Studies because God gives us the details of certain people to teach us and warn us for our edification.

Now all these things happened unto them for ensamples: and they are written for our admonition, upon whom the ends of the world are come.

1 Corinthians 10:11

Chapter 8

Bible Book Studies

Part 2

Biographical Studies

Another study important to a knowledge of a Bible book is a study of the persons of the book. Biographical studies start with the human author and extend to the various characters mentioned in the book. This is a gold mine of truth and blessing.

The aim of this study is to learn all of the facts about the person in question and to list those facts in a systematic way. Biographical studies are not difficult to do. The main thing is to *do* them – to work at it. The following form is only suggestive. There are actually many ways of doing a biographical study. Much of it depends upon the thoroughness of study and the imagination of the student.

1. The Person in Scripture

Using an exhaustive concordance (Strong's preferred), list all of the references to this person in the Scriptures. It is well to list them all at the very beginning of your study. Following that, you can look up each passage and study it. Check off each reference in your list as you look up the passage. Make notes as you read each of the passages. You can then use these notes in your final work.

2. Meaning of the Name

This is a good time to look up the person in a good Bible dictionary or encyclopedia. That way, you can find out if any other names have been applied to him or her. You can also find out a bit of data about the person. **Remember,** you have studied all of the references to that person first, and you have made your own notes. It is vital that you carefully study out every one of the passages of Scripture that you listed under #1 first. The Bible is the Source book which you must always search first. Dictionaries have been known to be superficial and misleading. As stated in the previous chapter, dictionaries often contain traditional ideas rather than Biblical fact.

3. Birth and Early Life

In this you are interested in background. These would be things which would help or hinder the relationship of this person to the Lord or his ministry. Also needed are things, which, though they might not help or hinder, would be of importance or merely of interest to your understanding of the person you are studying.

(1) Parentage (character and/or godliness of parents, religious upbringing, etc.)

(2) Place and/or circumstances of birth

(3) Early training and/or experiences

(4) Anything else which might be of help concerning birth and early life

4. Early Spiritual Experiences

Consider, as an example, the early experiences of Moses or of Paul. These experiences are very important to your study. As another example of this, consider the probable background of Timothy. Consider where Timothy came from and Paul's earlier experiences in that place. This would include —

(1) Conversion

(2) Call by the Lord to a specific task

(3) Other experiences showing an understanding or a lack of understanding, early spiritual errors or victories, etc.

5. Ministry for the Lord

(1) Nature of this ministry

(2) Reactions of others to that ministry

(3) Any prophetic mention as to the expected response

Example: God told Isaiah, Jeremiah, and Ezekiel what sort of results they could expect. See Isaiah 6 for one of these examples.

(4) Any prophetic utterances by this person in the course of his ministry

6. Character Evaluation

(1) Good

(2) Bad

7. Relationship with Others

8. His or Her Death and Comments about It

9. Why and How Is this Person Significant?

This would be the reason why we are studying this person in connection with the book or chapter in question. How does he or she relate to the passage? How does the expanded knowledge of that person help us to understand and appreciate the teachings of the passage that we are studying?

Example: In Jeremiah we find three sons of Shaphan, Ahikam who was father of Gedaliah (Jer. 26:24), a good man; Elasah (29:3); and Gemariah (36:10–12). It is not only interesting, but it is profitable to know more about each of these men, and especially to know who their father was. It helps one to realize the influence that a godly man has upon his sons. A study of some of Paul's companions (as in Col. 4) will yield many interesting and exciting insights as to the kind of men who traveled with him during those difficult but fruitful days. Paul lived in one of the most ungodly periods of history, but the Gospel was still his major subject of discussion.

Assignment

Choose a Bible character and make a Biographical Study of that person. Be sure to avoid picking someone like Paul or Moses for this study. The material on them would be too much to be developed in such a brief study. Do them later, if you like.

1. First, follow the system indicated in the divisions given above.

2. You may allow your imagination to govern anything more than this.

3. Be sure to use a work sheet (scratch paper) as you search out the information in the course of your study. Later you can bring it all together in its final form.

Work Sheet

Work Sheet

Work Sheet

Work Sheet

Work Sheet

What is God's Word?

1. It is a HAMMER — Jer. 23:29

2. It is a FIRE — Jer. 23:29

3. It is WATER — Eph. 5:26

4. It is a SWORD — Eph. 6:17; Heb. 4:12

5. It is SEED — I Pet. 1:23

6. It is FOOD — Heb. 5:12–14; I Cor. 3:2

7. It is LIGHT — Psalm 119:105

8. It is HONEY — Psalm 19:10

Looking Deeper into the Text

Part 1

Observation considers modifiers, verbs, nouns, and connectives.

Nouns give us who or what is the subject. Verbs gives what they are doing. Modifiers give us greater specificity about details. Connectives tie all the thought together correctly. Correctly understanding how these all work together is essential for accurate observation of scripture. Our goal is to follow Nehemiah's example when he opened scripture to Israel.

So they read in the book in the law of God distinctly, and gave the sense, and caused them to understand the reading.

Nehemiah 8:8

What does a modifier do?

A modifier qualifies, restricts, specifies, and limits.

Why is the study of verbs and nouns important?

The study of these gives us great insight into the passage by giving the core or "main stream of thought" of the passage.

Why should we learn about connectives?

They give us the relationship of words, phrases, clauses, sentences, and paragraphs.

Chapter 9

Looking Deeper into the Text

Part 1

1. MODIFIERS

In searching for the "core" of the Bible passage we often encounter many modifying words, phrases, and clauses, which we generally put aside in order to find the main "stream of thought" (or "core") of the sentence under consideration. These words are not put aside because they are unimportant to the passage. On the contrary, these modifiers are vital to an understanding of God's Truth, and we would be very foolish to ignore them. For that reason we now call your attention to this very necessary step in Bible study – a careful investigation of those terms.

To modify, in the *grammatical* sense, means "to qualify the meaning of, restrict; limit." The modifier specifies. Let us notice some illustrations of this:

Philippians 2:5, *"Let this mind be in you, which was also in Christ Jesus …."*

The term "mind" could refer to any mind: *my* mind, *your* mind, or Paul's mind. But it is not left to us to guess which, as this is specified by two modifiers: the word "this," and a clause, "which was also in Christ Jesus." (We must read on through verse 8 for a complete explanation.)

At times, great doctrinal truths may be seen in the modifiers. Our second example has to do with one of these:

Earlier we looked at the "core" of Hebrews 1:1–3. We may now proceed to find out even more from that analysis:

GOD

HATH
SPOKEN

BY HIS SON

WHO

being the brightness of His glory, and the *express image of His Person*, and upholding all things by the Word

of His power,
when He had by Himself purged our sins,

SAT DOWN

We have left out part of the passage for the sake of clarity. We will look at but one of the statements made about the SON WHO SAT DOWN: "Who, being … *the express image of His Person.*"

Express image (Greek, *charakter*) — Vine: "denotes firstly, a tool for graving (from *charasso,* to cut into, to engross; cp. Eng., character, characteristic); then, a stamp or impress, as on a coin or a seal, in which case the seal or die which makes an impression bears the image produced by it, and *vice versa,* all the features of the image correspond respectively with those of the instrument producing it…. (The Son) 'is both personally distinct from, and yet literally equal to, Him of whose essence He is the adequate imprint' (Liddon)." Christ bears the very stamp of God's nature.

The Son is an exact copy of the Father in His Person.

Person (Greek *hupostasis*) — Literally, "a standing under" (*hupo,* under, and *stasis,* a standing). The preliminary meaning includes the following:

"support," "existence or reality." The Stoics, who were Greek philosophers, used the word to denote, "what has come into being or attained reality." *Hupostasis* is "real being." In Hebrews, "transcendent reality" is closest to what the word means. Christ displays God's glory and bears the impress of the reality of God's being. Vine: "… here the word has the meaning of the real nature of that to which reference is made in contrast to the outward manifestation … it speaks of the Divine essence of God existent and expressed in the revelation of His Son." This same word appears in Hebrews 11:1, "Now faith is the *substance* of things hoped for, the evidence of things not seen." Faith is the "reality" (the substance) of things hoped for. Jesus Christ is the reality of the Father.

John 1:18 says, "No man hath seen God at any time; the only begotten Son, which is in the bosom of the Father, he hath declared Him." The word "declared" here is worthy of some study. Notice how these two passages complement each other.

2. VERBS AND NOUNS

It was necessary that some word studies be done in order to determine the "core" or main "stream of thought" of the sentence. Those word studies were specially limited to the verbs and nouns, and at that time, the essential message of the passage was found.

Now we go beyond the essential message and into other avenues of exploration of the verbs and nouns in a Bible passage.

Occasionally, finding the definition of a verb or a noun will yield some gem of truth which can be important to us in a doctrinal sense, or which will give a clearer understanding of the Scripture passage at hand. Most of the verbs and nouns are clear in the English. All we need to do with them is to meditate upon them a bit, asking questions, comparing parallel Scriptures, and drawing prayerful conclusions. In other cases, it is necessary for us to make a word study.

An illustration of this is seen in Romans 1:4. In our example we will leave out all but the parts which are essential to the illustration.

CORE:

WHICH

WAS MADE
and

DECLARED   ("to be" – italics)

THE SON OF GOD with power

BY THE RESURRECTION

from the dead.

The word *DECLARED,* a verb, is full of significance. Greek *horizo,* from *horion,* a boundary line. It means to mark out, to bound. To mark off by boundaries.

CAUTION: We must be careful about equating our word "horizon" with this word, saying that the Son appeared "on the horizon as the Son of God." We have heard some say that is what this verse tells us. The English word "horizon" comes from this Greek word — not vice versa. What is the horizon? The horizon simply marks the boundary of our vision. We cannot see beyond the horizon.

What then did the resurrection do? It "marked out" or "determined" Jesus Christ to be the Son of God <u>WITH</u> <u>POWER</u>. "*… it was not possible that He should be holden of it* (death)" (Acts 2:24b).

He brought to naught (nothing) "*him that had the power of death; that is, the devil*" (Heb. 2:14). See also Romans 4:25 and 5:10 which cast further light upon this subject. The study of this one word, "declared," opens a vast area of knowledge to the Bible student, and it should stimulate us to do even more research. This also clarifies an important doctrinal truth. For certain, such a study will create a greater appreciation for the Person of our Lord Jesus Christ. This is particularly true of the two examples given above.

A great number of other similar examples can be found. The student of the Scriptures must always be alert for those things which will deepen his understanding of the eternal and powerful truths of the Word of God. To miss these things, to be negligent, is to fail to "*rightly divide the Word of Truth*" (2 Tim. 2:15).

IMPORTANT: The Bible student who is not familiar with the original languages of the Scriptures (Greek and Hebrew) may do this particular kind of word study very profitably, as long as he or she is careful to avoid working beyond their personal knowledge and ability. The inflections of the verbs and nouns are not considered in word studies of this nature, but only the definition of the root meaning of the word. A number of books are available to students which can help them with the inflections. It was on page 22 where we said, "An inflection is a change of form in the terms to indicate case, gender, number, tense, person, mood, voice, etc. This would include conjugation of verbs, the declension of nouns, pronouns, and adjectives."

In keeping with our devotion to direct, inductive Bible study, and the use of only the *basic* helps, we urge the student to avoid the commentaries until all means of direct study have first been exhausted.

Summary

1. The specific meaning of the passage is further clarified by doing word studies of modifiers, verbs, and nouns.

2. Further, making comparison of other Scripture passages by means of cross references adds riches and depth to the study. The use of cross references will be developed even more later in our study. Your word studies frequently reveal other passages to study which may help you with an understanding of the truth of the passage you are studying.

3. Many important doctrinal distinctions are made clear through this type of study.

3. CONNECTIVES

It is necessary that you learn to take note of connecting words (or connectives). For us to make a thorough study of these words here and now would occupy considerable time and space. But they should be a big part of your study. You need to be conscious of connectives.

We will give this subject a brief look in passing, and assume that you will work at developing a sense of these important words. Some of them are short words, but size does not indicate importance. You need to learn to recognize them.

Connecting words are important because they show the following relationships:

- Comparisons and contrasts between words, phrases, clauses, and even between sentences.
- Conclusions drawn
- Progression of thoughts
- Logical relationships
- Cause and effect
- Chronological order
- To emphasize

Examples of connectives:

- *Therefore,* and *wherefore:* It has been said often in my hearing that "whenever you see the word *therefore,* you want to see what it is there for." The same is true with *wherefore.* These are connecting words and express conclusions drawn or the need for a conclusion to be drawn from the statement which precedes them.

  Note: Some have outlined the book of Romans using the word "therefore" to mark the points of division:

  1. Therefore of condemnation — 2:1
  2. Therefore of Justification — 5:1
  3. Therefore of Sanctification — 8:1
  4. Therefore of Consecration — 12:1

- *Furthermore* has to do with succession. This appears but three times in the New Testament, and in each case is translated from a different Greek word.

- *Moreover* is to be especially noted in I Corinthians 15:1. It refers to what has been said in Chapter 14, and it then indicates that Paul is taking us further. It says, "beyond what has been said." In that passage it comes from the Greek word *de,* usually translated "but." A little knowledge of Greek grammar would help here, however, you are encouraged to trust the King James translation. Let me explain: according to *A Manual Grammar of the Greek New Testament* by Dana and Mantey, this is a *postpositive conjunction* (post position, placed after). It is "(1) commonly used as an *adversative particle ... but, however, yet, on the other hand,* etc. (2) ... also common as a *transitional* or *continuative* particle, ... *and, moreover, then, now,* etc." Some contemporary translations have missed this. You can trust the King James Version.

- *For* appears many, many times in the Bible. It is always worthy of our complete attention. That is, be sure to see what it is "there for."

- *What then?* This appears in Romans 3:9. It is a connective calling for a conclusion to be drawn based upon what he has just said. Paul has raised a question for reflection. He then proceeds to draw the conclusion.

- *That* shows purpose. (This word can also *specify,* as "*that* man," and as such is not a connective.) See Colossians 1:10 and 2:2, and Philippians 3:10. This word sometimes appears in the King James Version with no *specific* Greek word to back it up. It was supplied by the translators, having been required by the grammatical construction of the passage.

There are also words other than the ones I have given above which are used to connect thoughts. You should try to develop a sense of which words are connectives and how they connect.

Connectives will often connect greater sections of chapters and even the entire Bible book. Though, more often the connection will be of thoughts within the sentence or the paragraph.

Within the sentences and paragraphs:

The relation of independent (coordinate) clauses to each other in compound sentences, and the relation of dependent (subordinate) and independent clauses in complex sentences are indicated, for the most part, by coordinate and subordinate connectives. Some of these are shown below. They have been divided into four categories and illustrative Bible references are given for each. The four categories are as follows: *temporal,* or chronological; *local,* or geographic (having to do with location); *logical,* and *emphatic.*

Temporal or *Chronological* connectives:

after	(John 13:5)
as	(Acts 16:16)
before	(John 8:58)
now	(Luke 16:25)
then	(I Corinthians 15:5)
until	(Mark 14:25)
when	(John 11:31)
while	(Mark 14:43)

Local or *Geographical* connectives:

Whither	(Hebrews 6:20)
Whence	(John 8:14)
Hence	(John 2:16; 14:31)
Thence	(John 4:43; Acts 20:15)

Logical connectives:

Reason —

because	(Romans 1:21)
for	(Romans 1:11)
even as	(Romans 1:28)
since	(I Corinthians 15:21)

Result —

so	(Romans 9:16; 1 Corinthians 8:12 and 14:25)
then	(Galatians 2:21)
wherefore	(I Corinthians 10:12)
therefore	(Galatians 5:1)
thus	(I Corinthians 14:25)

Purpose —

to the end	(Romans 4:16)
that	(Romans 5:21)

Contrast —

but	(Romans 2:8)
much more	(Romans 5:15)
nevertheless	(Romans 5:14)
else	(I Corinthians 14:16)
otherwise	(Romans 11:6)
yet	(Romans 5:7)

Comparison —

also	(II Corinthians 1:11)
as	(Romans 9:25)
as – even so	(Romans 5:18)
just as – so	(Romans 11:30–31)
likewise	(Romans 1:27)

Series of facts —

and	(Romans 2:17–20)
first of all	(I Timothy 2:1) — [Order of importance]
last of all	(I Corinthians 15:8)
or	(II Corinthians 6:15)

Condition —

if	(I Peter 2:3)
if – then	(Colossians 3:1)

Emphatic connectives:

indeed (II Corinthians 11:1)

only (Galatians 5:13)

— These were adapted from *Methodical Bible Study* by Traina, pp. 42–43. [He used the A.S.V. We have converted to the King James Version.]

Considerations in the above examples:

1. It is not exhaustive — others can be found — but it is typical.

2. The four main categories are not exclusive of one another. For example, a *temporal*

connective may also imply a *logical* relationship. Some of the same connecting words may also be found in more than one category.

3. Many of these same relations are to be found within clauses as well as between clauses, sentences, and paragraphs. The student must exercise discernment in determining the use of each connective.

4. The absence of expressed connections (a connective *word*) does not mean that the clause or sentence is not related. Comparison is frequently implied, even without a connecting word to show that relationship. Again, the student must develop discernment in this.

5. We can clear up many of the problems one may anticipate with connectives by saying, *"Use common sense."* A passage will make a statement. If we are to understand that statement, we must realize first of all that it is in the language which we commonly use. It matters little whether or not we categorize the connective as *temporal, local, logical,* or *emphatic.* What matters is that we, by using common sense, can grasp the statement. If you cannot, we have given you some tools in this course which should help you a great deal.

Assignment

1. Do word studies on the adjectives *merciful* and *faithful* in Hebrews 2:17. Write out a practical application to yourself as a believer.

2. Do a word study on *"made* Himself *of no reputation"*, Philippians 2:7. [Use *reputation* in Strong's to find the meaning. It is all one word.]

3. Pick 5 different connectives from any chapter of Philippians. Categorize each, and explain the connection.

Work Sheet

Looking Deeper into the Text

Part 2

Observation compares pertinent Parallel Scripture Passages.

We can best understand Scripture by comparing similar passages in the Bible.

Which things also we speak, not in the words which man's wisdom teacheth, but which the Holy Ghost teacheth; comparing spiritual things with spiritual.

1 Corinthians 2:13

What is the best commentary on the Bible?

The best commentary on the Bible is the Bible itself.

Observation studies with an inquisitive mind asking questions to stimulate thought.

God is pleased with our searching scripture with an inquisitive mind.

These [those in Berea] were more noble than those in Thessalonica, in that they received the word with all readiness of mind, and searched the scriptures daily, whether those things were so.

Acts 17:11

Why should we ask questions of the Bible?

Asking questions OF the Bible trains us to think and meditate on Scripture.

How can we keep the results of our Bible Study?

Use a simple, clear method of recording and filing your Bible Study Notes.

Chapter 10

———— ❧ ————

Looking Deeper into the Text

Part 2

1. PARALLEL SCRIPTURE PASSAGES

"There is no other commentary on the Bible so helpful as the Bible itself. There is not a difficult passage in the Bible that is not explained and made clear by other passages of the Bible ..."

> — R. A. Torrey in his Introduction to *The Treasury of Scripture Knowledge,* Fleming H. Revell Co., Old Tappan, NJ

"The Bible is the only commentary that is absolutely dependable. By comparing Scripture with Scripture ... we [can] become sure of the meaning of a particular passage. Our authority in all matters pertaining to faith and practice is not the teaching of isolated verses here and there, but the illumination and corroboration of the united testimony of all the Scriptures."

> — *How to Study the Bible,* Ed F. Vallowe, 528 Pine Ridge Drive, Forest Park, GA 30050

The Scriptures tell us to compare *"spiritual things with spiritual"* (1 Corinthians 2:13). The best way to do this is by comparing Scripture with Scripture. To study each Bible passage as if it were an isolated part is to make a most serious mistake. The Bible is *one* Book, and there is complete unity in its message, even though it was written by many men over a period of hundreds of years. It is "The Miracle Book of diversity and unity," as R. G. Lee would say.

When Jesus told the Jews, His people, to "*search the Scriptures,*" He went beyond that immediate occasion, for, if *we* search those same Scriptures, *we too* will find that they speak of Him. Jesus Christ is the Subject of the Bible! He fills its every page.

Kinds of Parallels:

There are many kinds of parallel passages to be found in the Bible. Here are some of them:

1. *Parallels in quotation:* There are passages which quote or refer to other passages of Scripture. Example: Psalm 110:1 compared with Matthew 22:43–44.

2. *Parallels of idea:* There are parallels showing a similarity of expression or of thought. Example: Ephesians 5:22 – 6:9 compared with Colossians 3:18 – 4:1.

3. *Parallels of enlargement:* There are parallel words, or terms, in which the meaning of the term is amplified and emphasized. Examples: "adoption," "election," "firstfruits," etc.

4. *Parallels of illustrative incident:* There are passages which illustrate and illuminate other passages using living illustrations. Example: Proverbs 24:16 with Esther 7:10; Proverbs 21:1 with Esther 6:1.

5. *Parallels of clarification:* There are parallels of doctrine which explain, enlarge, and clarify the doctrinal concepts. We have already seen some of these in our studies in this course. Example: The supremacy of Christ as shown in Hebrews 1, Romans 1, etc.

6. *Parallels of development:* There are parallels in which a Bible subject is developed completely. Example: Consider judicial blindness in passages such as Isaiah 6:9–10; Matthew 13:14; Mark 4:12; Luke 8:10; John 12:40; Acts 28:26; Romans 11:8 (considering the context in each, of course).

7. *Parallels of interpretation:* There are parallels which, through illustration or other means, enable us to understand a difficult passage.

8. *Parallels of fulfillment:* There are parallels which show fulfillment of prophecies, predictions, or of promised curses or blessings.

9. *Parallels of adaptation:* These are parallels which modify the original thought and exhibit it in relation to some new set of circumstances. Example: Jeremiah 31:15 compared with Matthew 2:17–18.

10. *Parallels of application:* There are parallels which enable us to apply a Bible passage by bringing its truth to bear upon some particular circumstances. Example: Matthew 2:23 and John 1:46.

Sources of Cross References:

1. The marginal references in a good reference Bible are most important as a source of cross references. We might add that the Scofield Reference Bible has only a limited number of cross references, since they use the reference column to follow their topics. These are helpful, and should not be rejected. I have an old Bible, now mostly fallen apart, which my Mother gave me for 8th grade graduation. It has a *treasury* of great cross references.

2. A concordance may be used to search out terms.

3. Personal reading and study is the best. An important habit to develop is the habit of noting parallel passages in the margin of your Bible as you notice them when you study, hear a message, or sit under a Bible teacher. We try to cover this in Bible Marking.

4. Commentaries and other helps provide many helpful cross references. In fact, I often look at the commentary more as a source of parallel passages than as a source of helpful comments. I have frequently done the same with books on theology or Bible doctrines.

5. An excellent source is *The Treasury of Scripture Knowledge,* a book published by Fleming H. Revell Co., Old Tappan, NJ. You will have to wade through much extraneous material to get the best cross references, but it is worth the effort to do so. The compiler of this book is unknown, but he, or they, no doubt compiled it from the works of others.

Rules for Using Cross References:

1. Search in the same book of the Bible first. *The Treasury* does this.

2. Search in other books of the Bible which were written by the same human author.

3. Find passages in other books of the Bible which were written during the same period of time or under the same or similar circumstances.

4. Finally, look anywhere in the Bible. It is one unit, a whole with many parts. We may trust it wholly.

2. ASKING QUESTIONS OF THE PASSAGE

> I have six faithful serving men
> Who taught me all I know.
> Their names are *What* and *Where* and *When*
> And *How* and *Why* and *Who*.
>
> —Rudyard Kipling

The Questioning Mind

The Bible student must train his mind to think. Asking the right questions is the principal means of stimulating thought.

Ask yourself these questions:

What?

What is it?

Where?

Where is it? Where did it come from? Where did it go?

When?

When did it happen? When will it happen?

[Place and time are always important in the study of the Scriptures. This is especially true of Old Testament studies. The geography and history of Paul's travels are not only interesting, but they are very helpful.]

How?

How did it happen? How will it happen?

Why?

Why is it as it is? Why will it be?

[Be careful when you ask why. Sometimes we can know the answer readily, more often we cannot. This does not mean that there are no answers to this question in the Scriptures. We must be careful about treading on sacred ground. Let God have his reasons, unless

He gives them. Never try to imagine motives in Bible characters unless they are given.]

Who?

Who is he? Who will it be?

Important: The Bible Holds the Answers

It is important to ask the questions of the Scriptures, but we must find our answers **only in the Scriptures** and not from other sources. The Bible is our guidebook. Only what is written in it can be trusted to be correct. Secular sources have been, and can be, doctored by all of the demons of Hell just so that man will go astray.

Commentators, though they are usually godly men, are fallible. I have a Bible Dictionary which has been recommended as being the finest. Yet, I have often found a *traditional* view presented rather than a Scriptural view. The Dark Ages were plagued by the allegorical method of interpreting the Scriptures. Men have a difficult time in ridding themselves of all that "baggage."

We must remember that the Christian's Textbook is God's Word. It is unchangeable, and sure forever.

— Proverbs 2:1–5:

> *"My son, if thou wilt receive my words, and hide my commandments with thee; ² So that thou incline thine ear unto wisdom, and apply thine heart to understanding; ³ Yea, if thou criest after knowledge, and liftest up thy voice for understanding; ⁴ If thou seekest her as silver, and searchest for her as for hid treasures; ⁵ Then shalt thou understand the fear of the LORD, and find the knowledge of God."*

The Bible student must approach the Bible in ways that are ever new. Every passage must be observed as if you had never seen it before, even if you might have read it a hundred times over. And you ought to refer to previous observations only *after* you have completed your latest *fresh* observations. We need to learn to ask honest, earnest, enlightening questions of the Bible. Do not ever fear that such questions will lead you astray. You may ask questions *of* God's Word, but you may **never ever** question God's Word! Its message is true, and Truth. It is God's Word to man.

Meditation:

— Psalm 1:1–2 (in part):

*"Blessed is the man ... [whose] delight is in the Law of the L*ord*; and in His Law doeth he meditate day and night."*

Meditation is thinking, and thinking is enhanced by asking the right questions of the passage. Meditation is also observing from many points of view. Meditation is *never* a mere *emptying* of the mind, as some believe they must do today. That sort of thing is dangerous, for if the devil can fill that mind, he can possess it! Biblical meditation means to *fill* the mind with God's Word, and to allow that Word to speak to us.

God's Word has energy, it works within us (1 Thess. 2:13). God's Word is alive ("*quick*"), it is powerful, it discerns our hearts (Heb. 4:12). The Word on the shelf does no good, but the Word in the heart does (Psalm 119:11).

The Bible student must learn to spend hours in prayerful study and meditation. This requires that we exercise self-discipline. It requires much patience. God always gives His very best to those who take time with Him. We may be like Martha, busy *doing,* or we may be like Mary, *sitting at His feet.* Jesus said, *"Mary hath chosen that good part, which shall not be taken away from her."* (Luke 10:42)

Helpful Hints in Studying Your Bible:

Some additional thoughts of things you can do which can be a help and a blessing for you. Along with what you have studied in this course, go through the passage and write answers to the following questions:

1. PERSONS OF THE PASSAGE

   (1) *Who Is speaking?*

   To whom does he speak?

   What is the reason for, or the occasion of, the speaking or writing?

   How many characters are revealed? (This will include groups.)

   (2) *God, or the Godhead:*

   Is God the Father mentioned?

   Is God the Son mentioned?

Is God the Holy Spirit mentioned?

What truths can we learn about God as He is mentioned in the passage?

What should be my response to each?

2. POINT OF THE PASSAGE

(1) *What is the main message or lesson?*

Is it as applicable today as when it was written?

Can I apply it to my life?

(2) *Is any prophecy (prediction) included?*

Is there fulfilled prophecy to strengthen my faith?

Is there any unfulfilled prophecy to enliven my hope?

(3) *Can I use anything from this passage in witnessing to or in helping others?*

(4) *What verse or verses should I memorize?*

3. HELPS IN RECORDING OBSERVATIONS

1. Always use a pencil as you observe. It is essential that you write things down if you are to study your Bible effectively. And by "effectively," we mean that you learn it.

2. You need to keep a notebook in which to record and file your observations. Loose scraps of paper are not much good. Some people like index cards. They do not work well for me. I prefer leafing through a notebook over fishing through a file. Besides, I can carry a notebook with me wherever I go. A card file takes up too much space, and I lose cards when I carry them separately. Also, cards are too small for notes. A notebook of 5¹/2" x 8¹/2" size is handy, since that size compares well with most Bibles. Many will even fit in a Bible case. I usually carry a few sheets with me in the fly leaf of my Bible. They don't fall out as easily as cards do. There will be more on this farther down.

3. Develop an electronic note keeping system. This will give you the greatest accessibility and flexibility for your notes. This could be a word-processing document on your computer or a study app that you can access on your phone, computer or the Internet.

Think through what you want it to do and try to explore a few options before you get set on one. Don't be afraid to learn something new.

Plan for a discussion of this in class.

4. Avoid too much detail in writing things down. Find ways of organizing the observations that you make as you study so they will be accessible later on.

Two goals should be kept in mind: Simplicity and clarity. Be thorough enough so that you will understand what you meant to say when you look back on your notes at some time in the future. But be concise enough for simple and quick review of your material. Much precious time can be lost in trying to figure out notes which have been made too hastily and carelessly.

Some suggestions for making notes of your observations:

(1) Separate everything by verse or by paragraph. If necessary, have a separate sheet of paper for each. Or, if you like index cards, have a separate card for each.

(2) Write down everything that occurs to you relative to the passage you are studying. Forget about logical order at this point. It can later be written in a logical sequence, and you should do so. Or, you can later number in the left hand margin to indicate the order. Use a felt tip or contrasting colors when you indicate order.

(3) It is wise to use sheets of paper (or cards) which are all of the same size, so they can be kept in some kind of order. To use scraps of paper, then to toss the whole mess into a folder or an envelope is not wise. I have previously mentioned notebooks or a card file. Remember that you are **now** beginning a lifetime set of Bible study notes which need to be kept in an easy to access format.

I personally recommend that all Bible study notes be kept in 5^1/2" x 8^1/2" ring binders (or 8^1/2" x 11"). Additional notes are easily added.

Using 5^1/2" x 8^1/2" size sheets fits easily in a Bible and extra sheets can be carried with you. These can be added to you notebook(s) by either Bible book or topic.

(4) Learn to use a medium pencil for marking your Bible neatly. Of course you would not use a hard pencil; that would ruin the pages, and it is difficult to see. Too soft a pencil will smudge and eventually blacken your pages.

There are many types of pens and marking devices available for Bible marking. These may be purchased on line or in Christian book stores. Make careful choices and learn a method of marking that will be understood and easily added to when you reread your Bible.

I have written a course on Bible marking called *Biblical Charagraphics - The Mechanics of Bible Marking*. In that course I warn against using a ball point pen to mark in your Bible. The ink in ball point pens is designed to not dry up. If it did, the pen would soon be useless. Thus, it will keep on soaking and soaking in your Bible until your writing is completely illegible. In my oldest Bible I marked with a red pen. Not only can you not tell what I wrote, but you cannot tell which page I wrote it on. It has soaked both ways over a number of pages.

Assignment

1. Make the suggestions in this chapter a part of your life.

2. Obtain a notebook (or a card file) and start to preserve the results of your Bible studies, of messages you hear, of lessons, or of anything that might be helpful.

3. Learn to apply the Scriptures to your life in every case. Three questions to ask when studying any passage:

   (1) How does my life compare?

   (2) What do I intend to do about it?

   (3) How can I go about obeying this passage?

Appendix 1

Worksheets

Main Truths Summary Example

Bible Study Worksheet

Name: _____ Ken Spilger _____

Quotation of the Passage	Outline of the Passage	Word Studies from the Passage
Passage: ___2 Timothy 2:2___ 2* And the things that thou hast heard of me among many witnesses, the same commit thou to faithful men, who shall be able to teach others also. 2* And <2532> the things <3739> that thou hast heard <191> (5656) of <3844> me <1700> among <1223> many <4183> witnesses <3144>, the same <5023> commit thou <3908> (5639) to faithful <4103> men <444>, who <3748> shall be <2071> (5704) able <2425> to teach <1321> (5658) others <2087> also <2532>.	1. The things that thou hast heard of me among many witnesses 2. The same commit thou to faithful men 3. Who shall be able to teach others also.	"that thou hast heard" - 191. ακουω akouo ak-oo'-o; a primary verb; to hear (in various senses):-- give (in the) audience (of), come (to the ears), ([shall]) hear(-er, -ken), be noised, be reported, understand. "witnesses" - 3144. μαρτυς martus mar'-toos; of uncertain affinity; a witness (literally [judicially] or figuratively [genitive case]); by analogy, a "martyr":-- martyr, record, witness. "commit thou" - 3908. παρατιθημι paratithemi par-at-ith'-ay-mee; from 3844 and 5087; to place alongside, i.e. present (food, truth); by implication, to deposit (as a trust or for protection):-- allege, commend, commit (the keeping of), put forth, set before. "to faithful" - 4103. πιστος pistos pis-tos'; from 3982; objectively, trustworthy; subjectively, trustful:-- believe(-ing, -r), faithful(-ly), sure, true. "able" - 2425. ικανος hikanos hik-an-os'; from ικω hiko [ikanw hikano or ikneomai hikneomai, akin to 2240] (to arrive); competent (as if coming in season), i.e. ample (in amount) or fit (in character):-- able, + content, enough, good, great, large, long (while), many, meet, much, security, sore, sufficient, worthy. "to teach" - 1321. διδασκω didasko did-as'-ko; a prolonged (causative) form of a primary verb daw dao (to learn); to teach (in the same broad application):-- teach.

Page: ___15___

Main Truths Summary Example

Cross References for the Passage	Questions about the Passage	Application of the Passage
Exodus 18:21 Proverbs 20:6 Luke 16:10-12 1 Corinthians 4:2 *Note: it is good to write the verses out*	**1. What things have we heard that we are to teach?** See 2Timothy 4:10. 10* ¶ But thou hast fully known my doctrine, manner of life, purpose, faith, longsuffering, charity, patience, 11* Persecutions, afflictions, which came unto me at Antioch, at Iconium, at Lystra; what persecutions I endured: but out of them all the Lord delivered me.	Will you give yourself to God to commit the things that God has taught you to faithful men who will teach others also? This is my commitment.
3. How do we commit them to faithful men? See 2Timothy 2:3-7. 3* Thou therefore endure hardness, as a good soldier of Jesus Christ. 4* No man that warreth entangleth himself with the affairs of this life; that he may please him who hath chosen him to be a soldier. 5* And if a man also strive for masteries, yet is he not crowned, except he strive lawfully. 6* The husbandman that laboureth must be first partaker of the fruits. 7* Consider what I say; and the Lord give thee understanding in all things.	**2. How do we know if they are faithful men?** See Luke 16:10. 10* He that is faithful in that which is least is faithful also in much: and he that is unjust in the least is unjust also in much. 11* If therefore ye have not been faithful in the unrighteous mammon, who will commit to your trust the true riches? 12* And if ye have not been faithful in that which is another man's, who shall give you that which is your own? 13* No servant can serve two masters: for either he will hate the one, and love the other; or else he will hold to the one, and despise the other. Ye cannot serve God and mammon. Continued... →	
4. How will they teach them to others also? See Titus 1:9. 9* Holding fast the faithful word as he hath been taught, that he may be able by sound doctrine both to exhort and to convince the gainsayers.		**Main Truth of the Passage** Successful ministry glorifies God by raising up godly generations who will reach the lost and teach the saved so that our whole society is impacted.

Bible Study Worksheet

Name: _____

Outline of the Passage	Questions about the Passage	Word Studies from the Passage
Passage: _____		

Page: _____

Cross References for the Passage	First Person Paraphrase of the Passage	Application of the Passage
	Main Truth of the Passage	

Appendix 2

Guide to Preparing Deeper Word Studies for Preaching and Teaching

There are times when it is necessary and beneficial for the Pastor or Sunday school teacher to provide more information than what is available in the dictionary found in Strong's Concordance. What steps need to be taken to satisfy that need and prepare a more complete word study?

1. Collect the necessary tools

The pastor/teacher will need at least the following tools in order to prepare a more complete word study: a good English language dictionary, **Strong's Exhaustive Concordance of the Bible** and **Vine's Complete Expository Dictionary of Old and New Testament Words**. Other books such as those mentioned in the last lesson may be helpful.

2. Look for the word in the English language dictionary

Write down all of the definitions provided. It will probably be necessary to eliminate as superfluous some of these definitions when writing the final version to be presented in public. We will use the word «transformed» as found in Romans 12:2 as an example of a more complete study. **Webster's New Twentieth Century Dictionary** provides the following definitions for the verb 'transform': "v.t.: 1. to change the form or outward appearance of; 2. to change the condition, nature, or function of; to convert; 3. to change the personality or character of; 4. in electricity, …; 5. in mathematics, …; 6. in physics, …; v.i. to be or become changed in form; to be metamorphosed. [Rare.]".

3. Look for the word in Strong's Concordance

It will be necessary to follow the steps presented in the previous lesson with an important change: instead of copying the information provided in the dictionary as is, write the information provided by Strong in a fluid manner. That will require the elimination of all abbreviations, putting complete words in their place, and adding words as needed to make the meaning comprehensible to the public.

'transformed': "(3339) metamorfóo; from 3326 (metá […]) and 3445 (morfóo: to fashion, figuratively); to tranform (literally or figuratively; metamorfose):—change, transfigure, transform".

4. Look for the word in Vine's Dictionary

Once the English word has been found in the dictionary, it will be necessary to search in Vine's dictionary for the original word examined in Strong's Concordance. You will notice that the information provided for the New Testament words is much more extensive than that provided for the Old Testament words; the portion of his work devoted to the Old Testament contains less than half of the Old Testament words. Write down all of the information provided in a manner that is easy to read. If Vine has written a comment specific to the text in question, take note of it in such a way that it stands out from the rest of the commentary about the word.

Found under transfigure "(metamorfoo, 3339), to change into another form (meta, implying change, and morphe, 'form:' see FORM, No. 1), is used in the passive voice (a) of Christ's 'transfiguration,' Matt. 17:2; Mark 9:2; Luke (in 9:29) avoids this term, which might have suggested to gentile readers the metamorphoses of heathen gods, and uses the phrase egeneto heteron, 'was altered', lit., 'became (ginomai) different (heteros)'; (b) of believers, Rom. 12:2, "be ye transformed," the obligation being to undergo a complete change which, under the power of God, will find expression in character and conduct; morphe lays stress on the inward change, schema (see the preceding verb in that verse, suschetamizo) lays stress on the outward (see FASHION, No. 3, FORM, No. 2); the present continuous tenses indicate a process; 2 Cor. 3:18 describes believers as being 'transformed (RV) into the same image' (i.e., of Christ in all His moral excellencies), the change being effected by the Holy Spirit."

5. Write down all texts where the same Hebrew, Aramaic or Greek word appears in the Bible

Example: the following appears at the end of the definition provided by Strong ":—change, transfigure, transform". These are words to which the original Greek word was translated as used in the *King James Version* of the Bible.

Write on the page of notes something like this:

Romans 12:2 — transformed 3339
    change –

    transfigure –

    transform –

The space left blank between the words is important because this is where you are going to write the texts that mention the *original word*.

Romans 12:2 — transformed 3339
    change – II Corinthians 3:18

    transfigure — Matthew 17:2; Mark 9:2

    transform — Romans 12:2

6. Write down all necessary observations about each one of these texts

It is possible, even probable, that not all of texts will help explain the meaning of the word being studied. These texts and commentaries about them will have to be eliminated in the process of preparing what is to be used in the presentation of what has been discovered, whether it be as part of a sermon or during a study.

Romans 12:2 — transformed 3339
    change — II Corinthians 3:18 – the child of God goes through a process intended

to produce a complete change from that which is associated with human glory to that which is divine, a change carried out by the Holy Spirit.

transfigure — Matthew 17:2

Mark 9:2 – Jesus appeared before His disciples drastically changed making Him and what He wore shine a brilliant white. This text does not appear to be beneficial to this study.

transform — Romans 12:2 – the verb is in the imperative mode; it is an order, something mandated to do, it is not an option.

7. Revise and write

(1) Revise everything you have written; mark clearly all of the information that will be useful as part of an explanation of the meaning of the word in question. It is absolutely necessary to be sure to take into consideration the context where the word is found.

(2) Write out whatever will be necessary to share with the congregation or the class. Be sure to include a practical application of the word in the message of the sermon or lesson.

The commentary to be shared during the sermon/teaching will depend upon the focus of the entire message. But it appears logical to me to include as a practical application something along these lines: "As an important part of his 'living sacrifice', God has commanded that all of His children go through a metamorphosis, a change produced in them similar to what occurs in nature. The Holy Spirit works in us as God's children to change the despicable 'worm' that we were into a beautiful 'butterfly' prepared to fly to heaven when the moment determined by our Father arrives, thanks to the changes carried out in our character and conduct."

8. How to go even further

There will be times when it will be useful to amplify the study to the other Testament. In this case, you will have to start by looking for the word being studied in the Concordance. Then write down all of the texts where the word appears leaving space to take the necessary notes and put beside it Strong's number that corresponds to that text. Later, look for the word in the original language that corresponds to that number, eliminating all of the words that have nothing to do with the original word as found before. From there, continue as in sections 3 through 6. It is necessary to be sure and not allow yourself to be deviated from the original purpose for the preparation of the study.

Neither of the two verses found in the Old Testament provide information pertinent to a study of the word 'transform', in part because the information provided is scarce.

~ Written by Clayton Livengood

Assignment

Prepare a more complete word study for one (1) of the following words found in The Epistle of Paul to Philemon (be sure to follow the instructions provided in this lesson, showing all of your work):

    1. (v. 1) fellow labourer

    2. (v. 7) bowels

3. (v. 8) enjoin

4. (v. 10) begotten